PHILADELPHIA EAGLES

Where Have You Gone?

PHILADELPHIA EAGLES

Where Have You Gone?

FRAN ZIMNIUCH

SPORTS PUBLISHING

Sports Publishing books may be purchased in bulk at special discounts for sales promotion, corporate gifts, fund-raising, or educational purposes. Special editions can also be created to specifications. For details, contact the Special Sales Department, Sports Publishing, 307 West 36th Street, 11th Floor, New York, NY 10018 or sportspubbooks@ skyhorsepublishing.com. Sports Publishing® is a registered trademark of Skyhorse Publishing, Inc.®, a Delaware corporation.

Visit our website at www.sportspubbooks.com.

10 9 8 7 6 5 4 3 2 1

Library of Congress Cataloging-in-Publication Data is available on file.
Series jacket design by Tom Lau
Cover photo credit Associated Press

ISBN: 978-1-61321-826-6
Ebook ISBN: 978-1-61321-846-4

Printed in the United States of America

Those who can, do.
Those who can't, teach.
And those who can do neither write about those who can do
and teach.

This is for all those who have taught me to write
and
encouraged me to do so.

It's also for Brent and Kyle.

CONTENTS

Acknowledgments vii

CHAPTER ONE: THE SIGNAL CALLERS 1

CHAPTER TWO: THE GROUND GAME 29

CHAPTER THREE: THE RECEIVERS.................................... 53

CHAPTER FOUR: THE KICKERS 83

CHAPTER FIVE: THE "O" LINE 97

CHAPTER SIX: THE CONCRETE WALL.............................. 123

CHAPTER SEVEN: THE MINISTER OF DEFENSE............. 129

CHAPTER EIGHT: THE DEFENSIVE LINE......................... 135

CHAPTER NINE: THE LINEBACKERS.................................. 155

CHAPTER TEN: THE SECONDARY..................................... 177

ACKNOWLEDGMENTS

When it comes to the Philadelphia Eagles, every fan has a favorite football player. Some of those favorites are members of the Pro Football Hall of Fame in Canton, Ohio, and others are waiver-wire acquisitions and free-agent signings. But over the course of a lifetime of being a sports fan, some players are just more memorable than others. Be it their on-field accomplishments, an offseason activity, an off-the-wall behavior, or a high school or college familiarity, some players just stand out. That's why these former Eagles are remembered here.

Success (or lack thereof) on the gridiron is an interesting concept. A pro football player who is perceived as not very good (or, in Philadelphia, as a "bum") is probably better than any football player you have ever seen. It is a case of degrees. To attain the dream of playing in the National Football League, that player is a very special athlete.

Success (or lack thereof) on the gridiron also means very little once the final whistle blows. No matter how good or bad a certain player may have been, they all have shared their skin, blood, sweat, and tears in an effort to fulfill their dreams. At the end of their playing days lies a bold new frontier, a new chance to make their mark on another of life's playing fields.

Some of these former players made their most memorable marks on the field, whereas others achieved their greatest moments and successes in life only after their football careers ended. The fact is that many have never known greatness, living their lives out of the spotlight following football. But no matter what, they did enjoy their moments in the sun, or on a frozen tundra, which is still frozen in the minds of their fans.

Philadelphia Eagles: Where Have You Gone? is one of my dreams come true. The players I spoke with all were outstanding athletes who had dreams of their own. Some came true, others didn't. But regardless of the level of their success, they were proud members of an organization that has the most loyal, demanding, vocal and sometimes frustrated fans in the National Football League.

The original release of this book back in 2004 came about thanks to the help of some wonderful people. The great Jim Gallagher, a fellow graduate of the late, great Northeast Catholic High School in Philadelphia, is a member of the Eagles Honor Roll. While he never played a down for the team, he was a fixture in the Birds organization from 1949 to 1995. During his tenure with the team, he worked with 17 head coaches and 12 owners, general managers, and team presidents in capacities that included director of public relations, personnel director, associate director of sales and marketing, and director of alumni operations/traveling secretary. Jim was kind enough to temporarily come out of his well-deserved retirement to help me with this project. As the late, great Philadelphia baseball icon, Richie Ashburn, would have said, Jim has a mind like a steel trap.

Philadelphia Eagles: Where Have You Gone? would have never happened without Jim Gallagher—not in 2004 and not in 2015. Thanks Jim. We old Falcons have to stick together!

The Eagles organization was also great to work with. In 2004 it was Derek Boyko and Scott Horner who made my life easier. In 2015 it was Anthony Bonagura. Thanks so much for your help.

One of the cool things about writing sports books is the fact that you meet and interact with players and coaches and management types who help you understand the topic and offer their unique perspective. But for me the fun didn't end there.

As someone who appreciates the written word and those who use words well in their writing, I also had the opportunity to include the input of the best football writer I've ever read—Ray Didinger. I have been fortunate enough to read his writing for most of my adult life. A member of the writer's honor roll in the Pro Football Hall of Fame in Canton, Ohio, Didinger covered the NFL for more than 25 years with the *Philadelphia Bulletin* and the *Philadelphia Daily News*. A regular panel member of Eagles Postgame live on Comcast SportsNet Philadelphia, he shares a panel with Michael Barkann, Brian Westbrook and former Pennsylvania governor and Philadelphia mayor, Ed Rendell. He has also authored books which include *The Super Bowl: Celebrating a Quarter Century of America's Greatest Game*; *Football America: Celebrating Our National Passion* (with Don Shula); and *The Ultimate Book of Sports Movies* (with Philadelphia sports personality Glen Macnow).

Ray was kind enough to take time from his busy schedule to talk with me about two of his favorite subjects and mine—pro football and the Philadelphia Eagles. While I might have my own thoughts and perspective on some of the players included in this work, Ray offers his perspective, knowledge, and experience which got him into the Hall of Fame. When you see Ray on television or listen to him on the radio, he comes off like a really good guy. I can attest to that. Ray Didinger is a class act and a good man. Thank you, Ray Didi.

And then there remains the quintessential Eagles fan—my friend, mechanic, financial advisor, philosopher and neighbor—Larry Leder. Larry gladly shared his volumes of stats, magazines, and directories as well as his personal perspective as a fan. He also shared memories of certain plays and particular players that also made my job easier.

There are also lots of long-term friends who are always there, like "Buffalo" Bob Scott; Bob Meizinger; Bob Smylie; Mark Turnbull; the world's greatest DJ, the lovely Angela Mason; my wonderful friend, Elissa Walker-Campbell, who has invited me many times as a guest on her fantastic show, the Big E Sports Show, on Yahoo radio; Jim Groff; Mike Green and my former editor at the *Providence Journal-Bulletin*, Bud Barker. Couldn't have done any of this without any of you!

The people at Skyhorse Publishing make writing fun. A big thank you is in order for my go-to person at Skyhorse, Julie Ganz. Absolutely could not have done any of this without her either!

Enjoy!!

Chapter One

THE SIGNAL CALLERS

RON JAWORSKI

When it comes to Eagles quarterbacks, few had the long and successful run that Ron Jaworski enjoyed in Philadelphia. After joining the club from the Los Angeles Rams in exchange for tight end Charles Young in 1977, Jaws spent ten solid seasons under center for the Birds.

There were better quarterbacks in the NFL, but not many. The Polish Rifle had a strong arm and good accuracy. There were bigger signal callers in the NFL, but when he needed to scramble to pick up a few key yards, Jaworski played as big as necessary. But in addition to his physical talents, it was his desire, dedication and fierce competitiveness that separated Ron Jaworski from the remainder of the pack.

He amassed seven club passing records, including completions, touchdowns and yards. The confidence that Coach Dick Vermeil showed in Jaworski was repaid time and again, most notably in 1980 when he led the team to Super Bowl XV against the Oakland Raiders, earned Player of the Year Honors and was an All-Pro selection.

"I think the world of the guy," said Hall of Fame writer and Comcast SportsNet Philadelphia commentator, Ray Didinger. "He was the perfect quarterback for Dick Vermeil's team. It was all about the team and not about the individual. Jaws was a real team guy. He truly didn't

Tony Duffy/Getty Images

#7 · RON JAWORSKI

Youngstown State • Hgt: 6-2 • Wgt: 196 • Born: March 23, 1951

Position: Quarterback
15-Year NFL Career
4,117 Att • 2,187 Comp • 53.1% • 28,190 Yds • 179 TDs • 164 Ints
Eagles 10 Years (1977-1986)
3,978 Att • 2,088 Comp • 52% • 26,963 Yds • 175 TDs • 151 Ints

care about his passing statistics. All he ever cared about was winning the game.

"The relationship between he and Vermeil was interesting. Vermeil was like a father to him. Ronnie lost his dad at an early age and Vermeil became a father figure to him. Dick influenced him both on and off the football field. Dick was tough on Ronnie, just like he was tough on everyone else. Jaws had a cannon of an arm, but didn't really know the quarterback position when he came over from the Rams. But Dick turned him from a thrower into a quarterback. Ron to this day says that his successes in life, not just in football but after football, are a result of all that Vermeil taught him."

A durable leader on and off the playing field, Jaworski played in 116 consecutive regular-season games.

"Ronnie J was like a guard who got to play quarterback," said teammate Jerry Sizemore. "What a competitor and what a nice guy. He fit right in and was an outstanding quarterback."

A young and untested quarterback when he arrived in Philadelphia, Jaworski had a huge supporter in Coach Dick Vermeil. The coach's belief in No. 7 saw him through some tough stretches, as very demanding fans wanting to see their young quarterback mature overnight. It made for some challenging times. But Jaws believed in himself as much as his coach did, and he became a steady, if not spectacular QB, as well as an unquestioned team leader.

"Jaws was like having another Dick Vermeil on the field with you," said receiver Mike Quick, who once teamed up with Jaworski for a 99-yard touchdown pass. "He was very, very smart as a player. I always knew when the ball would come my way. He was very good at reading defenses and getting the ball to the right hands."

As Jaworski's skills at the quarterback position blossomed, his leadership skills and physical and mental toughness became apparent. He may have been booed by Philadelphia fans at times in his career, but those tough critics also respect his character.

"In Philadelphia, toughness really matters," said Didinger. "People respect how tough Jaws was and that he never blamed anyone else. Part of the quarterback position is taking the bullet. You don't blame your offensive line, or a receiver who drops a pass. He never turned on a teammate and never turned on the fans."

His best year statistically came in the 1980 Super Bowl season when Jaworski had one of the best seasons a Philadelphia Eagles QB has ever had. He completed 57 percent of his passes for a career-high 3,529 yards and 27 TDs, also a career best.

Jaworski threw for 3,000 yards four times in his career and connected on at least 16 touchdown passes eight times. He was steady, durable and as tough a quarterback as there was in the National Football League.

"Ron was everything in terms of a team leader and quarterback," said tight end Vyto Kab. "He was a leader on the field with his performance, his preparation and his dedication. He was definitely in control. Off the field, he was very personable. Ron was the kind of guy who would make you feel comfortable whether you were a star or a guy who just made the team."

The desire of Coach Buddy Ryan to bring Randall Cunningham along as his quarterback resulted in Jaworski's playing time being cut, as he attempted just 245 passes in 1986. Clearly not in Ryan's plans, Jaws moved on to Miami in 1988 and Kansas City the following year before calling it a career.

After his retirement Jaworski maintained a high profile in the Philadelphia area with numerous business ventures and charitable causes. In 1991 he founded Ron Jaworski Management, Inc., a multifaceted company that not only manages his businesses and personal affairs, but also those companies and organizations with which he is involved.

His broadcast career with ESPN, NFL Films, and NFL.com has made him a well-known football analyst. He has been involved with the Arena Football League franchise in Philadelphia, The Soul, and also owns three businesses that fall under the Ron Jaworski Management umbrella— Valleybrook Golf Club, The Chateau Resort, and The Showcase Sports Apparel Store.

Where Have You Gone?

JEFF KEMP

W hen it comes to former Eagles quarterback Jeff Kemp, it seems
fair to say that the apple didn't fall far from the tree. While the
younger Kemp didn't have as much success on the football field as his
father—the late Jack Kemp, former Buffalo Bills standout QB and the
then-future vice-presidential candidate—Jeff Kemp does have the same
dedication to God, family and living life the right way.

"I always expected to play football my whole life because my dad had
done it," Jeff Kemp said. "We talked football a lot, but he never pushed
me into it. We'd throw the football a lot. I was 11 when he retired, so I
was pretty fortunate to have been able to go to War Memorial Stadium
in Buffalo and throw the football around with guys like Paul Maguire.

"I'm very proud of my parents. I have great parents in Jackie and
Joanne Kemp. They are a team. My mom deserves a lot of the credit for
my dad's being able to do what he did. I love the fact that my dad played
professional football and I am very proud of the type of athlete he was
and all he's done in public service.

"I played 11 years and never thought that I'd be a back up. I always
thought that I'd play regularly and get to the Super Bowl. I didn't think
like a back up."

During most of his career, Kemp was a back-up signal caller. But he
did have his moments in the sun with the Los Angeles Rams in 1984 and

Photo courtesy of the Philadelphia Eagles

#16 · JEFF KEMP
Dartmouth • Hgt: 6-1 • Wgt: 200 • Born: July 11, 1959

Position: Quarterback
11-Year NFL Career
916 Att • 479 Comp • 52.3% • 6,230 YDs • 39 TDs • 40 Ints
Eagles One Year (1991)
114 Att • 57 Comp • 50% • 546 YDs • 5 TDs • 5 Ints

with San Francisco in 1986. He was acquired by the Eagles during the 1991 season and saw plenty of action after going through a crash course in the Philadelphia offense.

"It was an amazing situation," he said. "I only had a few weeks there, but a ton happened. I was with Seattle and lost my starting spot and my job there on the same day, after an ESPN Sunday night game. The Eagles picked me up, and I had to learn the system with Zeke Bratkowski, one of the coaches. Randall Cunningham was hurt, Jim McMahon was hobbled, and Brad Goebel didn't have a lot of experience.

"I had a blast. It's an intense city. You play football for the pressure. We had some intense games there and I played a lot. In my first game I got a concussion. My wife and kids had just gotten there. The last four weeks I played more than anyone else. We lost to Dallas, but beat the Redskins, which is one of the greatest memories I have. We were getting snookered by Washington, which was my hometown team. But we got three touchdowns and a field goal in the second half to win the game."

The Eagles went 10-6 but missed the playoffs. Kemp came back to training camp in 1992 but lost his spot on the roster to David Archer. He returned home to the Seattle area waiting for an NFL team to call, which didn't happen. Although he did get an opportunity to sign with the Cincinnati Bengals the following summer, Jeff Kemp felt that it was time to move on.

"I feel it was like God crushed the need for football out of me," he said. "When I played I tried to make the team and the people around me better by trying to be a gutsy team member. My family, honoring God and treating people right mattered the most to me."

Following his career, Jeff Kemp became executive director of Washington Family Council, now Families Northwest, in 1993. He has used his leadership and speaking abilities to strengthen families, leaders and society by casting a vision for improving family life and fostering a marriage movement in Washington State. The team networks with leaders from all segments of society—business, community, church, government and media.

In 2012, Kemp joined Family Life, as a Vice President and Home Builder Catalyst. Family Life is a national ministry leader in marriage conferences, radio outreach and empowering resources to heal and strengthen family. As he speaks and trains throughout the United States, Kemp passes on dynamic lessons that he learned during his 11 years as a professional athlete.

The late Jack Kemp and Jeff are one of just eight sets of father/son quarterbacks to play in the National Football League. The others are Archie Manning and Peyton, as well as Eli; Bob Griese and Brian; Phil Simms and Chris; David Whitehurst and Charlie; Oliver Luck and Andrew; and Emery Nix and Kent.

Jeff and his wife, Stacy, live in Little Rock, Arkansas. They have four children—Kyle, Kory, Kolby and Keegan.

Where Have You Gone?

PETE LISKE

A graduate of Penn State, Pete Liske guided the Nittany Lions to Gator Bowl appearances in 1961 and '62 and was the MVP of the Hula Bowl Game following his senior year. After a brief stint with the New York Jets, he had a brilliant career in the Canadian Football league with the Calgary Stampeders. In fact, he won MVP honors in 1967.

Liske went back to the NFL in 1969 with the Denver Broncos for the 1969 and '70 seasons. The following season, he became the starting quarterback for the Philadelphia Eagles.

"We had a good run one year and finished up well," he said. "Then we stumbled the next year. But we had some big wins. We had a good group of receivers, Harold Jackson, Harold Carmichael and Ben Hawkins. Jackson led the league in receiving, so we had some success.

"Jackson was extremely quick and fast. He ran nice, quick routes and had good hands. Carmichael started out as a tight end. He was a helluva target. And Hawkins was the classic pro receiver. He ran great patterns and could make the great catches."

As was the case with most quarterbacks, Liske understood that the signal caller was often credited with the success of the offense as well as any failures they endured. All things considered, he felt the Eagles faithful were knowledgeable and fair.

AP Photo/Rusty Kennedy

#14 · PETE LISKE
Penn State • Hgt: 6-2 • Wgt: 200 • Born: May 24, 1941

Position: Quarterback
Five-Year NFL Career
778 Att • 396 Comp • 50.9% • 30 TDs • 46 Ints
Eagles Two Years (1971-1972)
407 Att • 214 Comp • 52% • 14 TDs • 22 Ints

"It was frustrating at times because we didn't have the success we would have liked," he said. "We probably had more downs than ups. But if you did well, the fans were with you. If not, they let you know about it. I always thought that Philadelphia was a fine city and that the fans were fair. Their passion for sports is well known."

Liske was well liked by his teammates, who admired his tenacity on the field.

"Pete wasn't like one of these guys with a Southern drawl," said former Eagles running back Lee Bouggess. "He was like a New York-minded guy. He was fun to be around. We used to talk before the game to come up with things to do if the game plan wasn't working well enough. Unlike a lot of quarterbacks, he never got angry if we messed up."

He was also the type of player who got the most out of his ability. It was that characteristic that helped make him an appreciated athlete in a tough sports town.

"Pete was a guy who had a good time playing football," said another former Eagle, Billy Walik. "He played at a certain level. His talent was limited, he was not a great passer or runner. But he made a helluva lot of progress with the talent he did have. Pete was a pretty good generalist out there."

Former General Manager Pete Retzlaff echoed those sentiments about the former Penn State QB.

"Pete Liske was a good quarterback," he said. "He was very intelligent. Unfortunately, we didn't surround him with a better ball club. He knew football very well and had won a championship in Canada."

After his playing days ended, Pete Liske got involved in the business world before returning to football as an official. He spent four years officiating in college followed by six years in the NFL. Because of his experience as a player, he had a unique feel for the game and for what the players were trying to accomplish. Liske felt very comfortable on the playing field.

But the league instituted a rating system that at times rewarded officials for making penalty calls rather than letting the game proceed at its own course. That caused this football purist to have some second thoughts.

"I got frustrated because you had officials looking for penalties to be rewarded for making what were considered correct calls," Liske said. "Officials weren't being taught how the game was played."

He then returned to the college ranks and became athletic director at Idaho from 1992 to '96 and at Toledo from 1996 to 2001.

He has also worked at his alma mater, Penn State, helping to secure donations and gifts for capital projects, endowments and special funds.

He hopes that Philadelphia fans will appreciate his efforts on the playing field.

"I always tried to be competitive and do a good job," he said.

DONOVAN MCNABB

There is little doubt that Donovan McNabb is the greatest quarterback in the history of the Philadelphia Eagles franchise. His numerous team records are an impressive indication of just how talented and durable a player he was. But McNabb also holds an unfortunate place in team history as well. Both he and 1960s running back Cyril Pinder were booed by the Philly Faithful before even appearing in a game.

Pinder was a second-round draft pick in 1968 out of the University of Illinois who was brought in as a replacement for the popular running back Timmy Brown, who was sent to the Baltimore Colts. As he was introduced before the start of a home exhibition game, the rookie was booed by the fans who were expressing their frustration over the trade of Brown.

A generation later, McNabb was a top signal caller at Syracuse and was considered one of the best quarterbacks in the 1999 NFL Draft. The Eagles held the second overall pick and the Philadelphia pundits and many of the fans were certain that the best player in the draft for the Eagles was Texas running back Ricky Williams. When the Cleveland Browns chose Kentucky quarterback Tim Couch with the first pick of the draft, the path was clear to make Williams an Eagle. But the team chose McNabb, which led to an ugly reaction by Eagles fans at the draft who booed the choice and the team's new quarterback.

Photo courtesy of the Philadelphia Eagles

#5 · DONOVAN MCNABB
Syracuse • Hgt: 6-2 • Wgt: 240 • Born: November 25, 1976

Position: Quarterback
13-Year NFL Career
5,374 Att. • 3,170 Comp • 59% • 234 TDs • 117 Ints
Eagles 11 Years (1999-2009)
4,746 Att • 2,801 Comp • 59% • 216 TDs • 100 Ints

"Don was a real good player," said Ray Didinger. "I was not surprised that Andy Reid drafted him. I was pretty skeptical, but we knew they were going to take him. The offense at Syracuse University was fairly simple. Reid's offensive system was more complex and pocket-based. I thought Don had a lot of ability and he adapted pretty well."

The Birds got the pick right. McNabb's career far exceeded the other top five choices in the draft. In addition to Couch going to the Browns, Oregon quarterback Akili Smith was the third pick on Draft Day by the Cincinnati Bengals, the Indianapolis Colts nabbed Miami running back Edgerrin James and with the fifth overall pick, New Orleans choose Williams.

McNabb went on to play 11 seasons as an Eagle and holds a plethora of Philadelphia records. Just some of his team records include career pass attempts (4,746); completions (2,801); career passing yards (32,873); passing touchdowns (216); career 300-plus yard games (27); NFL Championship Games (5); career game-winning drives (23); game-winning drives in a season (5), tying him with Norm Van Brocklin and Randall Cunningham; career wins (92) and games started at QB (142). That impressive résumé would certainly indicate just what a fantastic player he was. Certainly, a player such as McNabb would be a revered and popular figure in the City of Brotherly Love. But nothing is ever quite that simple in Philadelphia.

"He was a very good player," Didinger said. "The numbers he put up will tell you that."

Even though he led the Eagles to four consecutive NFC East Division championships, from 2001 to 2004, five NFC Championship games and a Super Bowl in 2004, the quarterback never received a sense of unconditional love from the city. There was the controversy about commentator Rush Limbaugh's comments during his short tenure at ESPN citing that the media was, "very desirous that a black quarterback do well." The comments came on the heels of an 0-2 start by the Eagles in 2003. McNabb simply wanted to play quarterback and not be involved in any such discussion.

Another controversy came with the addition of wide receiver Terrell Owens in 2004. He and McNabb were a lethal combination. McNabb threw for 31 touchdown passes that season, 14 of which were caught by Owens. The Eagles were edged in Super Bowl XXXIX by the New England Patriots, 24-21. McNabb threw three TDs that day, but also tossed three crucial interceptions, two of which were in New England territory and one of which was inside the Pats 20-yard line. He completed 30 passes for 357 yards, but the mistakes were what was remembered along with the painfully slow pace the offense showed late in the game. There are those who claimed that McNabb was ill and actually threw up during a late-game drive, a charge which was denied by both the QB and Coach Andy Reid.

The lethal McNabb-Owens combination turned toxic the following season in 2005. McNabb started the year on the injured list and Owens was publically critical of his quarterback since the Super Bowl loss. He suffered through an injury-plagued season that was cut short in mid-November. McNabb was out of the season, replaced by Mike McMahon, who went 2-5 in the starting role, with the Eagles ending the season at a disappointing 6-10 mark.

Injuries and inconsistent play began to beget McNabb from this point forward, but he was still a very talented signal-caller who was more than capable of carrying the team on his broad shoulders. He played well in 2006 before tearing his anterior cruciate ligament (ACL) in Week 11 against Tennessee. Backup Jeff Garcia replaced him and led the Eagles to the NFC East Division title. The Birds won a playoff game against the New York Giants before losing to New Orleans.

Following a non-descript 2007 campaign, the Birds rebounded in 2008. McNabb threw for 23 touchdowns and Philadelphia once again reached the postseason. They beat Minnesota in the wild card game and then upended the New York Giants to advance to the NFC Championship game. But they were defeated by the Arizona Cardinals, 32-25, ending any hope for a return to the Super Bowl.

Two thousand nine proved to be McNabb's last season as an Eagle. While he threw for 22 TDs and 10 INTs, injury and inconsistency once again was the norm. McNabb suffered a broken rib in the team's 38-10 opening-game victory over Carolina. Highly-touted Kevin Kolb played the next two games before McNabb returned for a match-up with Dallas in the season finale. The Birds, who owned an 11-4 record, were already sporting a playoff berth. But Dallas embarrassed the Eagles, 24-0, leaving Philadelphia with a 11-5 record and no first-round playoff bye. In the wild card game, Dallas completely outplayed Philadelphia en route to a 34-14 win.

Criticism of McNabb's play and seemingly careless attitude grew. In April of 2010, he was traded to the Washington Redskins in exchange for draft picks. After a promising start to the 2011 campaign for McNabb and his new team, he once again struggled and was benched by Coach Mike Shanahan.

Following that season he was sent to the Minnesota Vikings, where he reunited with former Eagles Offensive Coordinator, Brad Childress, who was then head coach of the Vikes. McNabb went just 1-5 as a starter and was benched in favor of rookie QB Christian Ponder.

When his career ended in 2011, McNabb ranked fourth all-time in career interception percentage of just 2.20 percent, behind only Aaron Rogers, Neil O'Donnell and Tom Brady. McNabb retired as an Eagle on July 29, 2013 and has had his No. 5 jersey retired by Philadelphia as well as Syracuse University.

He now serves as an analyst on the NFL Network and FOX Sports.

Where Have You Gone?

NORM SNEAD

W hen it came to talent, this Demon Deacon from Wake Forest
let it be known early on that he was blessed with all the tools
of a great quarterback. The only Wake Forest signal caller to earn All-
America honors, he was All-Conference three times. Snead was the
first round pick of the Washington Redskins in 1961 and became the
first-quarterback in the history of the NFL to start all of the games
during his rookie season.

Snead was acquired by the Eagles prior to the 1964 season in a
surprising trade along with DB Claude Crabb for QB Sonny Jurgensen
and DB Jimmy Carr. After the initial disappointment over being traded
passed, Norm Snead became a fixture in Philadelphia until 1970.

"I wasn't surprised at the trade," he said. "But I was a little disappointed because my parents had to drive another 90 miles to get to the
games from Newport News. I enjoyed Washington. It was a fun place to
play because of the Capital, the Kennedys and the political atmosphere.
I was young and impressionable and it was a new experience for me.

"But I loved Philly. It was a great town with great people, and it
was a great place to play. I lived around Rittenhouse Square and walked
everywhere. There were great restaurants, art galleries, parks. It was a
very nice place to play. I was young and excited about playing in Philly."

AP/WWP

#16 · NORM SNEAD
Wake Forest • Hgt: 6-4 • Wgt: 215 • Born: July 31, 1939

Position: Quarterback
17-Year NFL Career
4,353 Att • 2,276 Comp • 52.3% • 196 TDs • 257 Ints
Eagles Seven Years (1964-1970)
2,236 Att • 1,154 Comp • 51% • 111 TDs • 124 Ints

But except for the 1966 season when the team went to the Runner-Up Bowl in Miami, there were not nearly as many wins as Snead and his teammates would have liked. The fans often voiced their displeasure and the quarterback is often the focal point when the team succeeds, as well as when it doesn't.

"What people fail to realize is that football is really a team sport," Snead said. "You are only as good as the weakest player on your team. You don't win championships with weak players. Winning requires talent and luck. The quarterback gets what he deserves. If you get paid the bucks, you have to participate.

"We had good fans. What are the fans for? To support the team and they want a winner. If you do well they support you. They aren't any worse than any other town like New York or Washington. Nobody likes losing teams. But we always felt that we could win. We prepared to win. That's the way it was. I never went into a game thinking I was going to lose."

The team had an array of talented players on both sides of the ball. Snead was selected to the Pro Bowl three times, and he had some outstanding receivers like Ben Hawkins and Pete Retzlaff to throw to.

"Norm threw the best passes I ever caught," said Ben Hawkins. "He was a really good quarterback with a lot of great attributes."

He was a respected leader on the team who had a great talent.

"Norm Snead was a wonderful man," said free safety Bill Bradley. "What an interesting guy he, was and he was a pretty good quarterback. Norm was a pure pocket passer who was highly intelligent and fun to be around."

But it always seemed like something was missing on those Eagles teams. There was talent, but they came up short too often.

"If you think about it, they had won the championship in 1960," Snead said. "When that happens and you do well, you draft low. It just takes a while for the cycle to catch up. We were on that down cycle. We had some really good players, but not nearly enough of them."

Typical of Norm Snead's career was the 1967 season in which he completed a then-team-record 240 passes with 29 touchdowns. But he also threw 24 interceptions that season, the second highest single-season mark for an Eagles quarterback. Not a mobile signal caller, he was sacked 49 times for a loss of 369 yards that year. He was susceptible to a strong rush and the effect of major injuries to the offensive line. But he persevered and showed up every week, known for his fiery determination and guts.

Snead was dealt to the Minnesota Vikings following the 1970 season and played for another seven pro seasons and also was a member of the

New York Giants and the San Francisco 49ers. When he thinks of his career, he has no regrets.

"When I look back on my years in the game, it's something I'm proud of," he said. "I thought we contributed to the advances made in the game. It was all very positive for me. I played in great cities, played with great teammates and made some great friendships.

"It was worth the effort it took to play. People don't understand all of the work to keep in shape in the off season, or rehabbing from an injury. I had an ability, and it's not often you get to throw a touchdown pass in Yankee Stadium. It was exciting, challenging and required great discipline."

After his playing days ended, Norm Snead returned to Virginia and was employed at Newport News Shipbuilding, working at an Apprentice School where he was also the football coach for 10 years. He subsequently moved to Naples, Florida, and has worked in the real estate business.

"I'd just like to be thought of as a good teammate who could play the game," he said. "It was fun."

Where Have You Gone?

NORM VAN BROCKLIN

Although Norm Van Brocklin quarterbacked the Eagles for only three years, he certainly made his mark. "The Dutchman" guided the 1960 Birds to the NFL Championship with a 17-13 victory over the Green Bay Packers.

A fiery competitor and leader on and off the football field, Van Brocklin's veteran presence helped transform the Eagles from cellar dwellers to world champions. Nine years earlier, he led the Los Angeles Rams to football's promised land.

"He was a no-nonsense, team guy," said his former teammate, receiver Pete Retzlaff. "If you made a serious mental mistake on the field, he would send you to the bench. Norm was a coach on the field.

"In those days, quarterbacks called their own plays. He was a good strategist and a very gifted passer. He was very generous, but very strict as a quarterback. He was well organized and dedicated to football."

Van Brocklin got a late start to his college career as he served in the United States Navy from 1943 to 1945. He was drafted out of Oregon as a junior by the Rams in 1949 and left college to begin his pro career.

When he arrived in Los Angeles, Van Brocklin played behind future Hall of Fame signal caller Bob Waterfield. Gradually, he got to the point where he was splitting time with Waterfield. He won the passing title in 1950 and '52 and '54 with Waterfield capturing passing honors in 1951.

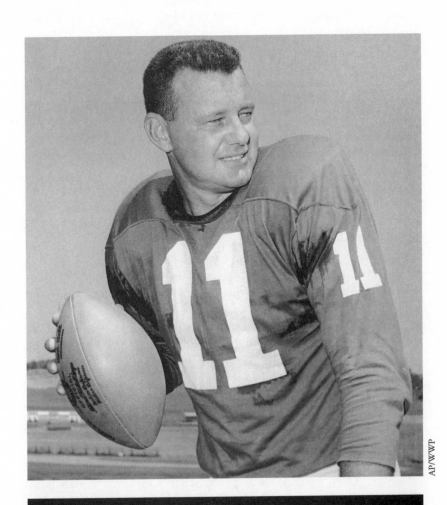

AP/WWP

#11 · NORM VAN BROCKLIN
Oregon • Hgt: 6-1 • Wgt: 190 • Born: March 15, 1926
Died: May 2, 1983

Position: Quarterback
12-Year NFL Career
2,895 Att • 1,553 Comp • 53.6% • 173 TDs • 178 Ints
Eagles Three Years (1958-1960)
998 Att • 542 Comp • 54% • 55 TDs • 51 Ints

Norm Van Brocklin was dealt to the Eagles in 1958 in exchange for Guard Buck Lansford, Defensive Back Jimmy Harris and a first-round draft pick. He became the first-string QB in Philadelphia under Coach Buck Shaw and carried the team on his shoulders without sharing time with another signal caller.

"I couldn't believe we got him from the Rams," said Chuck Bednarik. "He was the team leader, the most important player on the team. We felt like we were going to win with him. He was a real nice guy. But unfortunately, he retired after the 1960 season because he wanted to coach. I think we would have won again with him."

In addition to his quarterbacking chores, Van Brocklin also was the Eagles punter who twice led the NFL.

"He made us play at a higher level," said his former teammate Tom Brookshier. "Norm was in command. If you didn't play well, he would run you off the field and chew you out. If he had a bad game he would tell you that also. He wasn't afraid to pull himself out. He was a great guy personally. On Mondays after a game, he would call our homes and get our wives to get us out to meet him. Now where in the world could someone get a player's wife to tell you to go out and have drinks with the quarterback?"

The Dutchman, who played in 10 Pro Bowl Games, had one of his finest statistical seasons in 1960 throwing for nearly 2,500 yards in the 12-game regular season with a career-high 24 TD passes, good enough to earn the league's Most Valuable Player honors.

"If you look at the statistics, Donovan McNabb is the number-one quarterback in franchise history," said Ray Didinger. "But who played the position the best, at the highest level? To me, that is Norm Van Brocklin. No one ever played the quarterback position that well in Philadelphia."

In storybook fashion, both Van Brocklin and Eagles Coach Buck Shaw retired following the Birds' championship season of 1960, even though he was still at the top of his game. It was reputed that he had an agreement to become the Eagles coach when Shaw retired. Van Brocklin was supposedly unhappy that Assistant Coach Nick Skorich was promoted to the position.

Following that great season, Van Brocklin became a head coach with the Minnesota Vikings from 1961 to 1966 and with the Atlanta Falcons from 1968 to 1974. A respected coach, he amassed a 66-100-7 record with just three winning seasons in his 13-year coaching tenure.

"He was so brilliant strategically," said Tom Brookshier. "When he went into coaching I just wish that he could have gotten along with the players better. He had trouble with guys who didn't work as hard as he thought they should."

One of The Dutchman's most popular quotes was, "If I ever needed a brain transplant, I'd choose a sportswriter's, because I'd want a brain that had never been used."

Norm Van Brocklin was inducted into the Pro Football Hall of Fame in 1971.

Chapter Two

THE GROUND GAME

Where Have You Gone?

LEE BOUGGESS

When Lee Bouggess arrived in town as a third-round draft choice by the Philadelphia Eagles in 1970, he didn't really know what to expect. Then Eagles Coach Jerry Williams had scouted him in college at Louisville and took a liking to this hard-hitting running back. But for Bouggess, the big city seemed a long way from Kentucky.

"I guess I was a little shaky being a country boy," Bouggess said. "But it was a dream come true. Lenny Lyles, who was a defensive back for the Baltimore Colts told me how the fans gave a rough time to the players in Philadelphia. But my experience was really fantastic. I enjoyed playing and competing. Going against a guy like Dick Butkus who would growl at you from across the line of scrimmage. I was a physical running back. That's how I played.

"The people of Philadelphia loved me. The fans want you to put out every game. I was a hard-working person. The fans were very supportive. They were wonderful. I got invited to their block parties, people on the street were cordial. It all worked out great. Philadelphia is a great town."

As a rookie with the '70 Birds, Bouggess made an immediate impact rushing for 401 yards. He also caught 50 passes out of the back field, not a bad rookie season for a guy who was a defensive end until his senior year of college. That's when new Louisville Coach Lee Corso switched him to running back.

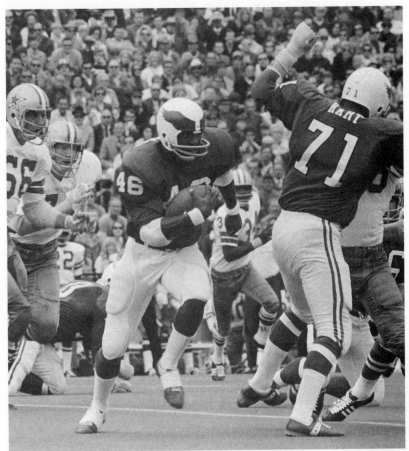

AP Photo/Ferd Kaufman

#46 · LEE BOUGGESS
Louisville • Hgt: 6-2 • Wgt: 215 • Born: January 18, 1948

Position: Running Back
Three-Year NFL Career
Eagles Three Years (1970-1973)
271 Rushes • 697 YDs • 2.6 Ave • 5 TDs

"He was asked to play a lot more as a rookie than anyone expected," said his teammate, wide receiver Billy Walik. "He had a great 1970 season. He was a hard-nosed player and a really nice fellow, too. Lee was a very goodnatured person. And the type of guy who you could trust."

Bouggess followed up with a strong sophomore season in Philadelphia but missed the entire 1972 season with a knee injury. When he returned the following year, he became a spot player, rushing the ball just 15 times and having only four receptions.

"Tom Sullivan was running the football then," he said. "Po James was doing really good. I got spot play and was just looking to get in the game. It didn't bother me splitting time. Sullivan gained over a thousand yards that year."

Bouggess was released the following training camp and caught on with the New York Stars of the WFL. The team then moved to Charlotte and had serious financial difficulties. At that point, Lee Bouggess decided to hang up his spikes and went to work for the Camden County Sheriff's Department.

He has worked for Gloucester County Parks and Recreation in Southern New Jersey, where he had served as assistant director. While his career ended sooner than he would have liked, Lee Bouggess has no regrets or second thoughts.

"I still miss it," he said. "But if I had only played in one pro game, I would have been satisfied. I got to run up the sidelines like Jim Brown. I got the opportunity to play professional football, and that's all I needed. It was a fantastic experience. There is nothing I'd rather do. If I had to play for free, I would have. That's how much fun it was for me.

"I tried to be the type of player they were looking for to take them to the Super Bowl.

LEROY KEYES

M arvin Leroy Keyes came to the Philadelphia Eagles as their first-round draft pick in the 1969 draft. Picked third behind O.J. Simpson and George Kunz, Keyes was picked by the Birds ahead of future NFL standouts including Joe Greene, Fred Dryer, Gene Washington, Calvin Hill, Bill Bergey, Ted Hendricks, and Ed Podolak. Hindsight is always 20-20, but at the time it would be difficult to fault Philadelphia for choosing Keyes.

A tailback and defensive back, he led the Purdue Boilermakers to the 1967 Big Ten Conference championship, was a two-time consensus All-American, 1967 Big Ten Most Valuable Player and runner-up in the 1968 Heisman Trophy balloting to Simpson. From 1966-68, Purdue had a 25-6 record with Keyes.

He notched several single-season records at Purdue, including rushing touchdowns (14 in 1968), rushing average (6.6 in 1967), points (114 in 1967) and touchdowns (19 in 1967). In addition, he is known for completing a 95-yard fumble return against Notre Dame in 1966 and for rushing for 2,090 yards in his Purdue career, including 1,000 yards in a season (1,003 in 1968).

So even though he wasn't O.J., he was certainly no lemon, either. But a preseason holdout and some good competition in the backfield made playing time difficult.

#20 · LEROY KEYES
Purdue • Hgt: 6-3 • Wgt: 212 • Born: February 18, 1947

Position: Running Back / Defensive Back
Five-Year NFL Career
Eagles Four Years (1969-1972)
123 Rushes • 368 YDs • 2.9 Ave • 3 TDs (29 Recep • 276 YDs)

So even though he wasn't O.J., he was certainly no lemon, either. But a preseason holdout and some good competition in the backfield made playing time difficult.

"My holdout didn't help out any," Keyes said. "You go in there with high ratings, but if the coach doesn't put you on the field, it's tough. Plus we had some good backs like Cyril Pinder, Harry Wilson and Tom Woodeshick. They didn't want me to be a marquee player.

"Things might have been different if Joe Kuharich had remained as coach. Leonard Tose bought the team and Pete Retzlaff became the GM. He was as hard-nosed a guy as I ever met. They brought in Jerry Williams, as quiet and naive a coach as I'd ever seen."

Keyes still showed his skill level as a rookie rushing for 361 yards on 121 carries for a 3.0 average and three TDs. An excellent receiver, he also caught 29 passes for 276 yards. But he ruptured his Achilles tendon toward the end of the year. That injury, the first of a number of setbacks, probably cost Keyes any chance of becoming an NFL star.

"I have no ill feelings toward anyone from my team in Philadelphia," he said. "I tore my Achilles tendon the end of my rookie year. If was a horse, I'd have been shot, so it could have been worse.

"After the injury, they moved me to free safety. I thought I had three good years playing with Nate Ramsey, Bill Bradley and Al Nelson. We did well. There were good folks on the team and we all competed. Just like the fans, we were exasperated by the losing. We wanted to win."

In spite of the disappointment over the way his career went, Leroy Keyes found a home in Philadelphia, a relationship that lasted long after his football career ended.

"I loved Philadelphia," he said. "I spent 27 wonderful years in Philadelphia. Most of my friends are still there. I'd still be there if Purdue had not offered me a job. I knew people like Ed Rendell before he was mayor, John Street before he was mayor. I had a chance to circulate in great circles. Philadelphia I loved.

"The fans are great. They support their teams, but they want winning teams. It's really a special town. I love the different geographic elements and parts of the city. Then you have one of the greatest zoos in the country. It's beautiful."

Keyes played with the Eagles through 1972 before finishing up the following year with the Kansas City Chiefs. While his career is considered mediocre by most, he still lasted for five NFL seasons in spite of numerous injuries. But people will always wonder what might have been.

"I would have liked to have gone to a couple of Pro Bowls and Super Bowls," he said. "But I just thank the good Lord for giving me the skills, the talent and the nerve to do what I did. Sometimes I sit in the dark and wonder what would have happened had I not gotten hurt. But I'm very thankful. Only a few people ever get to play in the National Football League.

"I did the best I could. I tried and didn't quit. I played hurt and ruptured my Achilles tendon two times. I hope my teammates appreciate what I tried to do, to be a team player who didn't make waves, and I tried to be a good force in the community.

"I'm not ashamed of my five years in the NFL. A long career wasn't meant to be. But I left some skin and blood on the field."

Following his playing days, Leroy Keyes stayed in the Philadelphia area and worked for the Probation Department in gang control before beginning a 17-year tenure with a school district as a desegregation specialist. But his alma mater came calling in 1995 and Keyes, Purdue's "All-Time Greatest Player" returned to the site of his greatest football accomplishments. He was named an assistant director of the John Purdue Club in July of 2000, a post from which he recently retired.

Previously, he served as administrative assistant with the football program from 1996-2000 and before that coached the running backs in 1994 and 1995, including All-America fullback Mike Alstott in 1995. Ironically, Alstott broke several of Keyes's Purdue records and finished as Purdue's career rushing leader with 3,635 yards.

Keyes was voted Purdue's All-Time Greatest Football Player in 1987 in commemoration of Purdue's Football Centennial Anniversary. He was also voted into the National Collegiate Hall of Fame in 1990 and was an inaugural inductee into Purdue's Athletic Hall of Fame in the fall of 1994.

WILBERT MONTGOMERY

No matter what Wilbert Montgomery did before or since, he will forever be remembered by Eagles fans for his performance in the NFC Championship Game victory over Dallas in 1980. All No. 31 did on that memorable day was rush for 194 yards, including his stunning 42-yard touchdown on the first play from scrimmage. That play and that game may well have been the top highlight for an entire generation of football fans in Philadelphia.

But more than a single play or game, Montgomery's entire eight-year tenure in Philadelphia was one that endeared him to the city. Though a smallish player, unimposing at 195 pounds, he played with an intensity not at all like his quiet and shy demeanor. He ended his career as the leading all-time rusher in Eagles history, surpassing the great Steve Van Buren.

Montgomery leads the franchise in rushing attempts with 1,465. A 1,000-yard rusher three times, his career best was 1,512 yards in 1979, his second consecutive Pro Bowl season.

Also a talented pass receiver out of the backfield, Montgomery caught 40 or more passes four times in his career, including 60 in 1984 and 50 in 1980.

Photo courtesy of the Philadelphia Eagles

#31 · WILBERT MONTGOMERY
Abilene Christian • Hgt: 5-10 • Wgt: 195 • Born: September 16, 1954

Position: Running Back
Nine-Year NFL Career
1,540 Rushes • 6,789 YDs • 4.4 Ave • 45 TDs (273 Recep • 2,502 YDs)
Eagles Eight Years (1977-1984)
1,465 Rushes • 6,538 YDs • 4.4 Ave • 45 TDs (266 Recep • 2,447 YDs)

"He was tough as nails," said teammate Mike Quick. "He took such a pounding, but he was relentless. Wilbert was very strong, fast and tough, a great, great football player. It was a pleasure to play with him."

He led by example on a team of leaders, a Reggie Jackson-like impact player with an equal amount of humility. His work ethic was second to none and he answered the bell no matter how nicked or injured he may have been.

"What a great guy Wilbert was," said offensive lineman Jerry Sizemore. "He was so quiet, one of those guys who didn't expect any attention. But he was so fast. No one cut back better. He worked really hard."

He retired as the 16th leading rusher in NFL history. After a fine 1984 season in which he rushed for more nearly 800 yards, he moved on to the Detroit Lions and finished up in 1985.

Montgomery has served as a coach for the St. Louis Rams (1997-2005), Detroit Lions (2006-2007), Baltimore Ravens (2008-2013) and currently the Cleveland Browns.

CYRIL PINDER

C yril Pinder had some pretty big shoes to fill when he arrived in
Philadelphia in 1968 replacing great running back Timmy Brown,
who was sent to Baltimore. A second-round pick in the draft out of
Illinois, Pinder was sandwiched between two Southern Cal picks of the
Eagles, Tim Rossovich and Adrian Young.

The Philadelphia teams of his era were a source of much frustration
for the fans as they accumulated considerably more losses than wins. It
was especially troubling because the team had talent.

"We had a great group of players," Pinder said. "No kick on our
coach Mr. Kuharich, but I think you have to handle men by treating
them as men. We had the talent and the capabilities. It just never came
together."

Pinder got spot duty that increased over time as he originally played
behind Tom Woodeshick and Isreal Lang. But his multidimensional
talent enabled him to run with power, run with speed and also saw
him become an outstanding receiver out of the backfield. As he became
accustomed to his increasing role on the team, Pinder also fit in nicely
as a teammate who really enjoyed the area.

"I loved Philadelphia," he said. "I was living at 2101 Chestnut Street
and just had a ball. I got married in '69 and we moved to Gypsie Lane

AP Photo/Larry Stoddard

#22 · CYRIL PINDER
University of Illinois • Hgt: 6-3 • Wgt: 222 • Born: November 13, 1946

Position: Running Back
Six-Year NFL Career
428 Rushes • 1,709 YDs • 4.0 Ave • 7 TDs (67 Recep • 556 YDs)
Eagles Three Years (1968-1970)
266 Rushes • 1,083 YDs • 4.7 Ave • 3 TDs (56 Recep • 492 YDs)

and started a new life. Philadelphia was a class, class organization. And it was a wonderful town."

During his time in Philly, Pinder was a popular member of the team where his abilities and personality were appreciated.

"Cyril is a guy that was a great running back," said former teammate Ben Hawkins. "He had a lot of ability and was a very powerful runner. We became good friends, and I think about him often."

After two years, Pinder became the team's leading rusher in 1970 gaining 657 yards with two touchdowns. He also caught 28 passes for nearly nine yards per reception. But contract negotiations with General Manager Pete Retzlaff went nowhere, and he was sent to the Chicago Bears in exchange for running back Ronnie Bull.

"I led the team in rushing and felt that I should get a bump in salary," he said. "Then they traded me to the Bears. It felt like I had been hit with a two-by-four. I cried for two days. I wasn't prepared to be traded. It's unfortunate that the Eagles never really utilized all of the skills that I had.

"Gayle Sayers's knee was not coming along as they had hoped, so Mr. [George] Halas traded for me. We had just moved into Vet Stadium. When I got to Chicago, the team was very polarized racially and otherwise. Abe Gibron was the coach and I was not his kind of guy. I think I asked too many questions. It was a terrible situation."

In spite of his inquiring mind, Cyril Pinder played well for the Bears rushing for 4.9 yards per carry in 1971 and 3.4 the following year. But his receiving ability went unnoticed and his disappointment over leaving Philadelphia never left.

"He is a man that demands and deserves respect," said former teammate Tim Rossovich. "We had a great deal of respect for each other. We pushed one another to make sure we worked as hard as we could."

After another unhappy year in Chicago, Pinder finished up his career with the Dallas Cowboys. But he realized that it was time to move on from football. He remained in the Chicago area and became an investment banker for 10 years. Now employed by the ABC Television Network, Cyril Pinder sells commercial air time to national accounts.

"I remember when I decided to retire, Roger Staubach couldn't believe it," he said. "But I decided it was time to utilize my degree and get into the mainstream of life. Football was a means to an end."

As a result of a botched extra-point attempt in 1972, Pinder is actually the answer to an interesting trivia question. With less than a minute remaining in a Bears game against the Redskins, he scampered for a 50-yard touchdown run to tie a game in Soldier Field. But after

Bobby Douglass fumbled the snap for the game-winning extra point, the southpaw quarterback spotted Dick Butkus alone in the end zone and passed the ball to him for a successful conversion. While most Bears fans remember the Douglass-Butkus hook-up, very few remember that it was Cyril Pinder who scored on the long touchdown run.

While his big play may have been overlooked in Chicago, Cyril Pinder never forgot his time in Philadelphia and the many friends he made there.

"I had so much fun when I was there," he said. "We had guys like Bob Brown, Ben Hawkins, Gary Ballman and Tim Rossovich. I gave all I could to the team and had talent which just wasn't utilized. I'd like to be thought of as more than a football player. I understood the game. But I just couldn't sell out all the way and commit my whole life to football."

Where Have You Gone?

STEVE VAN BUREN

When the Eagles drafted Steve Van Buren in the first round of the draft in 1944 out of Louisiana State, they knew he was a good football player. But as good as he was, it's impossible to predict a Hall of Fame career.

The Eagles had never finished above fourth place until Steve Van Buren came to town. His impact was felt immediately that year as they finished second, were runners-up two more years, won three straight divisional titles, and the NFL title in 1948 and 1949. Talk about making an impact.

He was a 1,000-yard rusher twice, won four NFL rushing titles and a rare "triple crown" in 1945 when he led in rushing, scoring, and kickoff returns. He was a first-team All-NFL selection each of his first six seasons. Van Buren lined up as a halfback but played more like a hard-nosed fullback as the battering ram of a powerful Eagles squad that dominated the NFL in the late 1940s.

"He was the best running back I've ever seen or played with," said former teammate Chuck Bednarik. "He was as nice a guy as he was a great football player. He was a quiet guy. Van Buren was strong, tough and really fast. He had that rare combination of quickness and strength."

Known as "Wham-Bam" by his teammates because of his quick and punishing running style, Van Buren led the Eagles to the National

Photo courtesy of the Philadelphia Eagles

#15 · STEVE VAN BUREN
Louisiana State • Hgt: 6-0 • Wgt: 200 • Born: December 28, 1920
Died: August 23, 2012

Position: Running Back
Eight-Year NFL Career
Eagles Eight Years (1944-1951)
1,320 Rushes • 5,860 YDs • 69 TDs (45 Recep • 523 YDs)

Football League championship in 1948, scoring the only touchdown in blizzard-like conditions against the Chicago Cardinals.

The following year, he rushed for 196 yards in rain and mud to help the Birds capture their second consecutive crown against the Los Angeles Rams.

Van Buren was the best running back of the 1940s, a worthy successor to the likes of Jim Thorpe and Bronko Nagurski. His power-running style was similar to later strong backs like Jim Brown and Jim Taylor. Van Buren was a no-nonsense, up-the-middle runner with enough speed to make a cut on unsuspecting defenders and enough power to run over them.

Steve Van Buren was born in Honduras, orphaned as a young child and sent to New Orleans to live with his grandparents. He failed to make the high school football team as a 125-pound high school sophomore, but as a senior he played well enough to win a scholarship to LSU.

In his senior season, Van Buren rushed for 832 yards. Encouraged by LSU coach Bernie Moore, the Eagles selected him as their top pick in the draft. It was a break for Van Buren and, for the Eagles, possibly their most fortunate ever.

Steve Van Buren died on August 23, 2012 in Lancaster, Pennsylvania of pneumonia.

Where Have You Gone?

BRIAN WESTBROOK

At 5-10, 203 pounds, Brian Westbrook is on the small side for a professional football player. He also played at a Division 1-AA school in Villanova, that has not historically been a football factory for the NFL. But success is success, and he had enough success during his college career to become the all-time NCAA record holder with 9,512 all-purpose yards. It's a mark he still holds.

That kind of production on the football field would make most pro scouts foam at the mouth. But his size, his school and the fact that he missed a season due to a knee injury kept him off of the must-have list of most pro teams. But Eagles Coach Andy Reid had seen Westbrook play a number of times and was impressed with his ability and confident that he could make the adjustment to the pro game. As a result, Philadelphia drafted Westbrook in the third round of the 2002 NFL Draft.

Westbrook was used sparingly in 2002, rushing 46 times for 193 yards and adding 9 pass receptions for 86 yards. He saw his workload in Reid's offense increase the following season, rushing for 613 yards on 117 carries (a career-high 5.2-yard average) with seven TDs. He also caught 37 passes for 332 yards and another four scores.

A true triple threat, Westbrook was a dangerous return man, a valuable featured back and a dynamic pass receiver. And he was sure-handed. In his nine-year professional career, he fumbled just 3 times in 1,385 carries.

Photo courtesy of the Philadelphia Eagles

#36 · BRIAN WESTBROOK
Villanova • Hgt: 5-10 • Wgt: 203 • Born: September 2, 1979

Position: Running Back
Nine-Year NFL Career
1,385 Rushes • 6,335 YDs • 4.6 Ave •41 TDs (442 Recep • 3,940 YDs)
Eagles Eight Years (2002-2009)
1,308 Rushes • 5,995 YDs • 4.6 Ave • 37 TDs (426 Recep • 3,790 YDs)

Westbrook quickly became a fan favorite in the sometimes difficult Philadelphia landscape. In fact, he received write-in votes in the 2003 mayoral election in Philadelphia. He also received write-in votes for State Supreme Court Justice, Superior Court Judge, Traffic Court Judge and Registrar of Wills. "That's great," he said of his ballot box breakout. "Maybe one day I'll decide to switch careers, but for now, I'm happy as an athlete."

That happiness reached new levels in 2004, which saw Reid and the Eagles reach the Super Bowl. Westbrook rushed for 812 yards during the regular season, but also caught 73 passes, giving quarterback Donovan McNabb another dangerous receiver in pass patterns. While the Birds were edged by the Pats in the Super Bowl, Westbrook rushed for 44 yards and added seven receptions for 60 yards.

The following season was marred by an early holdout and then an injury that limited him to parts of 12 games, but Westbrook returned to form with a passion in 2006. It marked his first 1,000-yard season on the ground, rushing 240 times for 1,217 yards. He also caught an amazing 77 passes for an additional 699 yards. Westbrook led the team with 11 touchdowns.

Brian Westbrook had one more remarkable season in him. In 2007, he rushed for a career-high 1,333 yards on 278 carries and 7 TDs. He also caught a career-high and franchise-record 90 passes for 771 yards and five more touchdowns. This premier back had more than 100 combined rushing and passing yards in 12 of his 15 games. Not only that, but he led the league with 2,104 yards from scrimmage. Needless to say, he was a first team All-Pro selection.

But the wear and tear had begun to take its toll starting in 2008. Nagging injuries limited his playing time, which saw him rush for 936 yards and nine TDs. He caught 54 passes for an additional 402 yards and 5 more scores. The injury trend continued the next season when he missed 8 games with two separate concussions.

Westbrook was released by the Eagles on March 5, 2010. He did play one more season, finishing his career in San Francisco with the 49ers in 2010. He rushed 77 times for 340 yards and had 16 receptions for 150 yards.

Westbrook has been a regular contributor on the Eagles Postgame Live TV show, which airs on Comcast Sportsnet following the games. He appears on a panel with host Michael Barkann, former Pennsylvania Governor Ed Rendell and NFL Hall of Fame writer Ray Didinger.

When he is not broadcasting, odds are that you will find No. 36 at the Westbrook Horse Farm in Upper Marlboro, Maryland. As passionate about horses as he was about football, Westbrook founded the farm in 2006. It has grown from the original 25 acres to 50 acres of fenced pastures, wide open fields and wooded areas.

Chapter Three

THE RECEIVERS

Where Have You Gone?
_____

GARY BALLMAN

The Philadelphia Eagles franchise has been blessed with some outstanding receivers. Quality players such as Tommy McDonald, Ben Hawkins, Pete Retzlaff, Harold Jackson, Harold Carmichael and Mike Quick, are just a few examples of outstanding targets for Eagles quarterbacks.

In the late 1960s, Gary Ballman was as dependable as any of the above. A two-time Pro Bowl performer with the lowly Pittsburgh Steelers, he had the opportunity to play with some tough football players in the Steel City.

"We beat the crap out of everybody, but didn't win too many games," Ballman said. "Buddy Parker was the former coach of the Detroit Lions and he picked up all the bad-assed players on waivers. We were sort of like an early version of the Oakland Raiders. We came close, but never really had the attendance to go out and get anybody."

Ballman was acquired by the Eagles prior to the 1967 season in exchange for Bruce Van Dyke and Earl Gros. Ballman contributed some solid seasons to the team, snaring 166 catches in six years.

"When I came to the Eagles, Joe Kuharich was the coach," Ballman said. "I played under him at the East-West Shrine Game and the Hula Bowl. Five years later, we had the identical play book. Everyone else in

Photo courtesy of the Philadelphia Eagles

85 · GARY BALLMAN
Michigan State • Hgt: 6-2 • Wgt: 194 • Born: July 6, 1940
Died: May 20, 2004

Position: Receiver / Tight End
13-Year NFL Career
Eagles Six Years (1967-1972)
166 Receptions • 2,379 YDs • 15 TDs

the league was doing shifts and motion, but we didn't have any of that. It was sort of like damn the torpedoes and full speed ahead.

"Coming to Philadelphia, the team had a decent record. We felt that we would be a contender. But losing was quite frustrating. I think I had all the capability in the world. But I played with something like 25 quarterbacks in 12 years. I never had the time to develop a rapport with a quarterback and get the timing down. The exception to that was Bobby Layne with Pittsburgh. He could throw the football and hit you perfectly in stride."

Ballman was a versatile performer who played as a wide receiver and also at tight end for the team. He was also adept at returning punts and kickoffs. The Michigan State graduate also became very fond of Philadelphia and the fans.

"Philly was great," he said. "There are some of the greatest restaurants in the world there. We used to love Bellmont Hills and the Bocce Club. It was a very entertaining place. And you could take the train and get just about anywhere.

"The fans were typical. If you win they love you. If you don't, they boo you. It's that simple."

Ballman was one of the more popular players on the team. He caught 36 passes in 1967, 30 in '68 and 31 the following year. His best year with the Eagles was 1970 when he caught 47 passes, equaling his career high, for 601 yards.

But by 1973 a serious knee injury helped end Gary Ballman's career in which he distinguished himself as one of the NFL's best pass receivers with 323 catches for more than 5,000 yards.

Following his career, Ballman went to work for the National Football League Players Association for a number of years. He then moved to the Colorado area where he was a salesperson in the building materials industry, prior to his retirement.

The NFL is a different game today, something that was not lost on Gary Ballman.

"It's boring, man," he said. "Everybody plays the same game. The offense is the same with every team, the San Francisco offense. They come out and pass, pass, run. That's it. It's mostly short passes, and the backs have to have very good hands as well."

Ballman was a popular figure in Philadelphia long after his time in the city ended. He was proud of his accomplishments on the football field.

"I'd like to be remembered for what I did," he said. "A lot of people don't know I did kickoff returns. I think I'm still fourth or fifth in average yards returned. I made the Pro Bowl a couple of times for Pittsburgh, which is tough if you're not from a winning team."

Gary Ballman died of a massive heart attack at his home on May 20, 2004.

Where Have You Gone?

BEN HAWKINS

The thought of Ben Hawkins in a Philadelphia Eagles uniform brings back memories that flash through your mind like speedy No. 18 would flash through opposing defensive coverage. A big play receiver who had a talent for getting open, Hawk always played with his chin strap dangling off of his helmet that hung over his shoulder pad as he broke free of defenders.

Coming out of Arizona State, Hawkins was drafted by the Eagles as well as the AFL New York Jets. A native of North Jersey, he decided the best place for him was Philadelphia. It's a decision he does not regret.

"I was a Giants fan growing up," he said. "I was in the last class of the combined draft and just thought it would be better to go to Philadelphia. Even though I was a New York guy, it was the right decision after everything was said and done.

"I liked Philadelphia. It was a big town with a small-town atmosphere. I still have a lot of fond memories of Philly and the fans. I look back very fondly on my time there. I enjoyed the city and met a lot of good people there."

Even though the Eagles did well in his rookie season of 1966, Hawkins had a disappointing year with just 14 receptions. As the team began to sink in the standings over the next few years, he established himself as one of the premier receivers in the National Football

Photo courtesy of the Philadelphia Eagles

#18 · BEN HAWKINS
Arizona State • Hgt: 6-1 • Wgt: 185 • Born: March 22, 1944

Position: Wide Receiver
Nine-Year NFL Career
Eagles Eight Years (1966-1973)
267 Receptions • 4,764 YDs • 32 TDs

League. In his sophomore season with the Birds, he nabbed 59 passes for 1,265 yards and 10 touchdowns.

"My first year was horrible," he admitted. "I couldn't catch a cold. But I was a decent player coming out of college, where I played behind Charlie Taylor. Based on the guys before me who made it in the pros, I felt I was good enough. I came back my second year to prove that the first year wasn't really me. I led the league in yards and was fifth in receptions. I was able to turn everything around. I think it was just a matter of more concentration."

His signature look with the dangling chin strap was just something that began in college and continued in Philadelphia. His play made him an inviting target for an NFL quarterback.

"Ben was the classic pro receiver," said Pete Liske. "He ran great patterns and had been a great player for a long time. And he could make the great catch."

Even though he became one of the best in the business at his position, the continued losing took its toll. But Ben Hawkins was a popular player with the fans of Philadelphia because he never gave anything less than his best.

"In the beginning it's something just to be able to play pro football," he said. "After a while, especially after coming from winning teams in college, it gets kind of hard. But you have to remain focused on what you do. I tried to focus on doing my part of the job and hoped that other things would come around. It just never seemed to jell after that first year. It's a struggle when you lose."

The fans often vented their frustration on the players during his tenure in Philadelphia. But Hawkins was a fan favorite who appreciated the knowledge and passion of the Philly faithful.

"They were good fans," he said. "They love their Eagles and live and die with them. They just let you know how they feel. The fans always treated me well. They really understand their football. I'll never forget the day in Franklin Field when they pelted Santa with snowballs at half time."

His NFL career effectively ended when he suffered a serious broken right leg in 1973. He was cut the following training camp and played briefly for Cleveland 1974, the Philadelphia Bell the following year and retired from the game when he failed to make the Eagles roster in '76 under Dick Vermeil.

"Ben was a great receiver," said Norm Snead. "Had great speed and great hands. He was loose and went across the middle. He was fun to play with and had fun playing, and I like that."

During his playing days, Ben Hawkins was a popular player in the clubhouse as well as in the stands. He was the consummate team player.

"Ben Hawkins changed my whole life," said former running back Cyril Pinder. "He was as flamboyant as anyone I had ever met. He drove an Astin Martin and had an apartment with a pool table. For some reason he befriended me and we became very good friends. He was the coolest guy I ever met and a great receiver. Ben was a super athlete."

After his career ended, Hawkins then coached for a number of years at Arizona State, the Eagles and San Antonio and Arizona of the USFL. What followed was a successful career working in management for a trucking company.

During his tenure in Philadelphia, Ben Hawkins was a force to reckoned with on the field and a visible and popular figure in the community. But although he had a great time, he never crossed that line that so many athletes now ignore.

"It's a good life that you lead," he said. "You are doing something you really enjoy and getting paid for it. You can have lots of fun, but you have to be careful, too. People look at you as a role model.

"You have a certain obligation to do what you're supposed to do every day. You understand what's right and wrong and try not to do the wrong things. That's what you want to teach the kids."

VYTO KAB

When Vyto Kab was drafted by the Eagles in the third round of the NFL draft in 1982, he was in a comfortable situation. As a native of the New York area, he felt at home on the east coast. And as a graduate of Penn State, he was on familiar turf.

"Playing at Penn State, it seems like you are either a Steelers fan or an Eagles fan," Kab said. "Being drafted by the Eagles and Dick Vermeil was something. I made the transition right into the NFL without too much difficulty. Playing at Penn State, most of our offensive players got drafted into the NFL. We had a pretty competitive team that played at a high level. Of course, the pros were an even higher level."

A hard-nosed player who left everything on the playing field, Kab was one of Vermeil's guys and a fan favorite. Like many players, while he adapted to being a professional football player, he also developed an appreciation for Philadelphia.

"It's my favorite town," he said. "There's no middle ground there. They love you or they hate you. I really enjoyed it there. I grew up in the New York area, and so much goes on there. There is not as much focus on football as there is in Philadelphia. When the Eagles were winning, you knew it. Playing there was a terrific experience. The town was great, very exciting. It has kind of a small-town atmosphere."

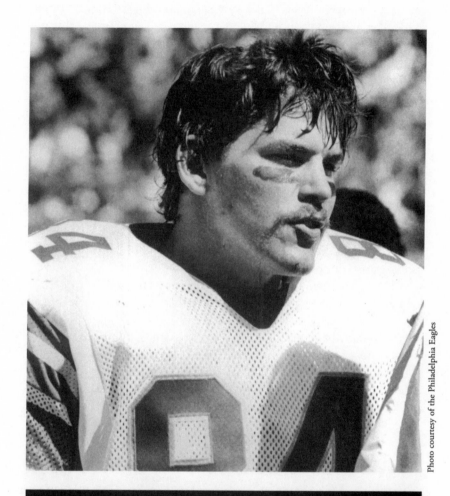

Photo courtesy of the Philadelphia Eagles

#84 · VYTO KAB
Penn State • Hgt: 6-5 • Wgt: 245 • Born: December 23, 1959

Position: Tight End
Five-Year NFL Career
36 Receptions • 386 YDs • 5 TDs
Eagles Four Years (1982-1985)
31 Receptions • 332 YDs • 5 TDs

Being a dependable player, even though Kab backed up John Spagnola at tight end, there were opportunities for him to play. After catching four passes in his rookie campaign, he nabbed 18 receptions in 1983. The following season, while he only caught nine passes, three of them were for touchdowns.

"They called my number a lot," he said. "Playing tight end, there are a lot of opportunities, particularly around the goal line. I was never a big-time receiver who would catch 90 balls. But down close, you force things and I was able to do it."

After splitting the 1985 season between the Eagles and Giants, things were looking up as far as Vyto Kab getting some more playing time. It appeared that he would finally become a starter in the National Football League.

"My last year with Detroit, I actually was slated to start at tight end," he said. "I just took it to a different level as far as getting ready for the season was concerned as far as working out and getting prepared to play. I got in the best shape of my career. Then in the last preseason game against Tampa Bay, I blew out my ACL.

"I enjoyed playing in the league. It's very challenging to play as long as I did. I enjoyed the relationships I made, some of which I still have today.

"I hope to be remembered as a dedicated professional as a player. I was someone who gave 110 percent and acted and played like a professional. I learned more about that after leaving the Eagles. About how different levels of being disciplined and different levels of being focused can help you increase your productivity."

Since his career ended, Vyto Kab has been nothing but productive. After working for a pharmaceutical company which led to working with respiratory equipment, he and his wife started their own business in 1993.

Kab was co-founder and co-managing director of SleepTech LLC and SleepTech Consulting Group, LLC. He was responsible for organizing and managing a ground-breaking study of the prevalence of sleep apnea in professional football players, cited in *The New England Journal of Medicine*. SleepTech, LLC, has grown to be one of the largest operators of AASM-accreditation level hospital-based sleep centers on the East Coast.

SleepTech Consulting Group works with organizations concerned with the relationship between sleep and the productivity of their employees, manages clinical trials and develops innovative continuing medical education programs.

"Sleep apnea is a closing of your airways when you are in a deep sleep," he explained. "Your breathing stops and you wake yourself up. That's what is happening when someone is snoring, snorting and waking up out of a deep sleep. Your oxygen levels go down and your heart rate increases. It can be disruptive to your health by causing hypertension.

"We are also showing the correlation between proper sleep and how you feel during the day. The research we're involved in is really interesting and gratifying. We can help a lot of people."

Kab sold the company in 2005. He is now a principal with Regent Real Estate Partners, developing medical office buildings and working with hospitals and doctor groups.

KENT LAWRENCE

H is lone NFL reception with the Eagles in 1969 may not have been memorable to most Eagles fans, but his outstanding college career at Georgia and his life of achievement following his football make Kent Lawrence a person worth remembering.

Stricken with rheumatic fever as a young boy, Kent Lawrence was told that he'd never be able to play sports. But he battled his way at every level of athletics with an intensity that belayed his slender frame. When the Eagles drafted him in the ninth round of the draft, the former Bulldog brought some impressive statistics and success from his college years.

A member of Coach Vince Dooley's championship teams at Georgia in 1967 and '68, Lawrence finished his college career with a 4.1 yards rushing average, gaining 922 yards with eight touchdowns. As a receiver, he caught 47 balls for 646 yards and as a kick return specialist, he is seventh on the SEC all-time punt return list with 795 yards, good enough for a 22-yard average. His accomplishments led to his induction into the Georgia Bulldogs' Football Hall of Fame.

The 1966 SEC championship team was Lawrence's first varsity season. It was one he'll never forget. "It was incredible," he said. "We couldn't play on the varsity until we were sophomores in those days. The chemistry on the team was unbelievable. We had good athletes on that

Photo courtesy of the Philadelphia Eagles

12 · KENT LAWRENCE
Georgia • Hgt: 6-0 • Wgt: 175 • Born: June 3, 1947

Position: Wide Receiver
Two-Year NFL Career
Eagles One Year (1969)
1 Reception • 10 YDs

team, but we were not blessed with a whole lot of stars. But there were a lot of athletes committed to success.

"Coach Dooley was one of those coaches who turned over responsibility to his assistants. He had great coordinators and assistant coaches. But he was in control. Everyone had tremendous respect for Coach Dooley."

Those successful years at Georgia were nothing like Kent Lawrence saw in his lone year with the Eagles in 1969. The Birds finished 4-9-1 under new Coach Jerry Williams, and Lawrence saw little action.

"Everyone with the team was great to me," he said. "Coach Williams; Pete Retzlaff, the general manager; and Leonard Tose, the new owner, was very friendly. The veterans kind of give the rookies a hard time but then they adopt you and look after you. I was real friendly with George Mira and Chuck Hughes, the receiver, who later died on the field when he was with Detroit.

"I enjoyed pro football, maybe not as much as college football. It was a whole different experience, more like a business. Maybe I wasn't mature enough to appreciate the pro game. I was never really intent on playing pro football for the rest of my life. I did it for the enjoyment of the game. That year with the Eagles I didn't find that the chemistry was there. I was glad to play and enjoyed the experience."

Lawrence made it to the final cut in 1970 and played with the Atlanta Falcons until a hamstring injury ended his season. Football began to take a back seat in his life as he was already working on his master's degree in education, which was followed by a law degree. He was public safety officer at the University of Georgia, an investigator for the Western Georgia Judicial District, police chief, an attorney, assistant solicitor for the state court of Clarke County and a judge for the state court of Clarke County.

"I never had a goal to be a pro football player," he said. "It was like the icing on the cake after being thought of as too small. It was a blessing that allowed me to walk away from professional sports. That is such a distant part of my life now.

"We have five children, and when I was inducted into the Georgia Hall of Fame at the Cotton Bowl in Dallas, they showed film clips of all of us. My kids were there and it was the first time they had seen me play football. It meant so much to me, because it meant a whole lot to them. I'm glad they got to see me play."

While not many people saw Kent Lawrence play in the National Football League, he made it to that level. He appreciates his NFL career as well as his alma mater, the University of Georgia.

"I would hope to be thought of as a competitor who was told by doctors that I wouldn't be able to play sports," he said. "The University of Georgia gave me an opportunity to get a quality education. I will always be indebted to them for allowing me to come here as a student-athlete. What's most rewarding today is being able to contribute something back to the community."

After twenty-six years on the bench, Judge Kent Lawrence retired on November 30, 2011 to spend more time with his family.

Where Have You Gone?

MIKE QUICK

A photo album could be overstuffed with highlights from the career of Mike Quick. The book would include many exciting, breathtaking receptions as well as the catches that NFL receivers are supposed to make. His 99-yard touchdown hook-up with Ron Jaworski ranks as one of the single most explosive plays in the history of the franchise, and he had great individual game performances throughout his career.

But no group of pictures can adequately tell the story of just how good and dependable the first-round draft pick from North Carolina State really was. His rookie season saw him play occasionally, catching 10 passes during the year. The professional game was quite different from the college game.

"You have to make big adjustments," Quick said. "The biggest one is the information you have to know. You have to be professional in what you do on the field and then as a young man who didn't have two nickels to rub together in college, you can all of a sudden purchase what you want. It was not an easy thing. People, I think, expect too much out of kids coming out of college to the pros. They are not ready.

"For me, I really focused on being successful at my job. You learn what you had to learn to be successful as a professional athlete. All of the knowledge of the defenses you are facing in the pros is much more

Photo courtesy of the Philadelphia Eagles

#82 · MIKE QUICK
North Carolina State • Hgt: 6-2 • Wgt: 195 • Born: May 14, 1959

Position: Receiver
Nine-Year NFL Career
Eagles Nine Years (1982-1990)
363 Receptions • 6,464 YDs • 61 TDs

complicated in college, reading defenses, making adjustments at the line and anticipating what the defense is going to do.

"My rookie season I got screamed and yelled at by Dick Vermeil a lot. Unfortunately, I only spent one year with Dick. Out of the twenty-two years I played football, that one year I probably learned more about the game than in the whole other twenty-one. He stressed being prepared and helped me take off in my second year."

And take off Mike Quick did, as he grabbed 69 passes in his sophomore campaign for a career-high 1,409 yards and 13 touchdowns. It was the first of five consecutive Pro Bowl selections that tabbed him as one of the premier receivers in the National Football League. Following his breakout second season, he followed with 61, 73, 60 and 46 receptions over the next four seasons.

But while Quick blossomed into an athletic, graceful and very successful receiver, the Eagles suffered through some difficult seasons.

"I wasn't happy because we didn't win a lot," he said. "We all were frustrated, because you want to play in the Super Bowl. But we didn't do well as a team and had three head coaches in my nine years there. It was not a stable situation.

"If the team is doing well you don't have to concern yourself with how you are doing personally. But I had to take solace in having good seasons."

There were countless highlights to Mike Quick's career, but he has a special memory that meant more to him than anything that occurred during his days as an Eagle. It began with a serious injury.

"This may sound corny, but I broke my leg against the Houston Oilers in '88 or '89," he said. "I had to go up to make a catch because it was a high pass, and I broke my leg before half time. After the half, I wanted to watch the second half from the field, and when I came out of the tunnel, the entire stadium stood up to give me an ovation. I had goosebumps all over me.

"That show of appreciation was my greatest moment. I appreciate how the people appreciated me. It was a great feeling."

Quick was a fan favorite, which not every Philadelphia Eagles player can say. But you could see Mike Quick's determination and professionalism with every play, regardless of the score or the team's record.

"I just played," he said. "I loved it, and it showed that I loved it. I enjoyed what I did and didn't take anything for granted. Even as a number-one draft pick, I worked my butt off to get better every day. I give respect to people and when you do that, you get respect in return.

"The fans care. You get some cities where the fans really don't care what's going on. With these fans, they are right there. Yeah, they boo. But when there is something to cheer about, they go crazy and cheer."

Quick played through the 1990 season before retiring. He has been involved in corporate work as a spokesperson and ambassador for some companies in the Philadelphia area. He has also distinguished himself as an honest, interesting and credible color commentator for Eagles radio broadcasts for seventeen years.

"My career was very special," he said. "Nearly every boy who plays sports as a kid dreams about playing professionally. I'm one of the few who had the opportunity to live my dream. I realize it and I'm very thankful."

PETE RETZLAFF

Throughout the proud history of the Philadelphia Eagles franchise, it is literally impossible to find a more respected person and consummate professional than Pete Retzlaff. Held in high esteem by teammates and opponents alike, it wasn't just the football success that Pete Retzlaff enjoyed, but his demeanor on and off the field that made him stand out.

Picked off the waiver wire by the Eagles from the Detroit Lions, who drafted him in the 22nd round of the NFL draft in 1953, Retzlaff retired as the Birds all-time leader in receptions with 452, receiving yardage with 7,412 and added a resounding 47 TDs. Not too shabby for a guy who was drafted out of South Dakota State as a running back.

"I was drafted by Detroit and went to training camp," Retzlaff said. "They had two veteran fullbacks on the team, and the odds didn't look good. So they had me start working with the receivers. When I got to Philadelphia, they didn't know what the hell to do with me. During one training camp they switched me back to running back, and I led all ground gainers. Then they put me back as a receiver."

During his first two seasons in Philadelphia, No. 44 saw little action catching a total of just 22 passes in two seasons. But beginning in 1958, Retzlaff became a force to be reckoned with in the National Football League catching 56 passes for nearly 800 yards. What a difference a year

George Silk/Time Life Pictures/Getty Images

#44 · PETE RETZLAFF
South Dakota State • Hgt: 6-1 • Wgt: 210 • Born: August 21, 1932

Position: Wide Receiver / Tight End
11-Year NFL Career
Eagles 11 Years (1956-1966)
452 Receptions • 7,412 YDs • 47 TDs

makes. Not to mention what a difference a quarterback with confidence in you makes.

"That was the year that Norm Van Brocklin came in. He told some people that he thought I reminded him of Elroy Hirsch, because of the way I ran pass patterns. I had a quarterback who had confidence in me, and that makes a big difference."

The confidence that Van Brocklin had in Retzlaff helped mold the team into championship form.

"Pete wasn't playing much before Dutch came to town," said Tom Brookshier. "He looked like Mr. Universe and was just being used part time and on special teams. Dutch started throwing to him and working with him. He felt that Pete could lead the league in receiving. Van Brocklin saw that ability in Pete, who was so strong and ran great pass patterns."

With great players like Van Brocklin, Retzlaff, Ted Dean, Chuck Bednarik, Tom Brookshier and a host of others, the Eagles captured the NFL championship in 1960 by defeating the heavily favored Green Bay Packers. Retzlaff caught 46 passes that year for 826 yards and five touchdowns. He was established as a premier receiver and Philadelphia was king of the football world.

"At the beginning of that season, nobody was picking us to do anything," Retzlaff said. "We lost the first game of the season to Cleveland at Franklin Field, then won nine straight to win the division. In that season in every game we won except one, we trailed at half time. Our team had a great deal of confidence in a quarterback named Van Brocklin."

Known as the Baron during his playing days, Retzlaff continued to be a dominant receiver who fit nicely in Philadelphia. Being an NFL player was quite an on-field adjustment for a small college player.

"Only two teams had helmets with logos in those days, the Philadelphia Eagles and the Los Angeles Rams," he said. "Philadelphia is a fantastic sports town. The fans are rabid. If you lose they'll string you up, but if you win, you can't pick up a check in a restaurant for a year.

"We were a Division 2 team at South Dakota State. It was quite a step up to the NFL when you realize you are suddenly on a team where most of your teammates were either All-Conference or All-American. There were loads of talent and your first reaction is that you'd better have something in reserve, because this is really a big step up."

No one can accuse The Baron of not stepping up. During the early to mid-1960s, he was one of the elite receivers in the game. But after a strong 1966 season in which he caught 40 passes and scored six touchdowns, Retzlaff retired, as his heart and mind were no longer in the game.

"Pete was probably the best prepared football player I knew," said Norm Snead. "He was strong, and his work ethic was unbelievable. He could run a pass pattern better than any receiver I ever played with. It's a crime he's not in the Hall of Fame. He certainly had the statistics."

A stint as a broadcaster was followed by four years as the Eagles' general manager. That is a tenure that Pete Retzlaff has had plenty of second thoughts about.

"It's too bad that you don't have the opportunity to make two decisions sometimes," he said with a chuckle. "Leonard Tose was very generous, but very difficult to work for. There can only be one authority figure in the office at one time. It was chaos when I was there.

"I can judge talent, but it's difficult to put the right team on the field with the right attitude. We inherited some players who weren't interested in dedicating themselves to winning football games. I tried it and was glad to leave."

Retzlaff has subsequently been involved in agriculture with farming interests in Nebraska, North Dakota and Texas.

He doesn't need to be remembered for anything but being an average guy. Or as he put it, "Just as a guy who hasn't died."

Where Have You Gone?

BILLY WALIK

Philadelphia sports fans in general and Eagles fans in particular are known for being tough on athletes. If a player gives it his all, the fans are appreciative pretty much regardless of the outcome. But heaven help the player who the fans think is giving less than everything he's got.

While he only played with the team for three years, Villanova grad Billy Walik won over the hearts of the Eagles faithful because of the exuberance and enthusiasm with which he played the game. Relegated to a back-up role because the Birds had three outstanding receivers in those days, Walik was an outstanding punt and kickoff return specialist.

"Back then, at most, teams played with three wide receivers," said Walik, who now answers to Bill. "I played behind Harold Jackson, Ben Hawkins and Harold Carmichael, who were without peer during that time. I played behind three of the greatest receivers in Eagles history. So I was relegated to returning kickoffs and punts. I had run a little track at Villanova and had good acceleration, which is the essence of a good kick returner."

Playing for teams that were not all that successful during his three seasons, going a combined 11-28-2, Walik had lots of opportunities to return kickoffs. He returned a career-high 32 in 1970, averaging 25.2 yards per return. That figure went up to 26.4 the following year.

Courtesy of the Philadelphia Eagles

#9 · BILLY WALIK
Villanova • Hgt: 5-11 • Wgt: 172 • Born: November 8, 1947

Position: Receiver / Punt & Kickoff Returns
Three-Year NFL Career
Eagles Three Years (1970-1972)
2 Receptions • 15 YDs • 1 TD
28 Punt Returns • 130 YDs • 4.6 Yard Average
67 Kickoff Returns • 1,640 YDs • 24.5 Average

"Billy was one of the fastest white guys I knew," said his former teammate, running back Cyril Pinder with a chuckle. "He had a tough chore to break into a lineup with some great receivers there. But he had talent and was good on special teams. He was a true professional."

One of Walik's fondest memories was the infamous *Monday Night Football* game of November 1970 that saw the Eagles defeat New York Giants. That was the game that saw a tipsy Howard Cosell get sick in the broadcasting booth in very close proximity to Don Meredith. In the HBO movie about Cosell, Walik's name is the only name mentioned.

"That was the night we beat the Giants and Howard Cosell got sick after having entirely too many martinis at a pregame party," Walik said. "That was a great memory along with when Bill Bradley and I lived in one of those row homes on the other side of the Vet Stadium parking lot. There was a hole in the fence that was part of our commute to a game or practice. We were just like kids sneaking into the park."

His old buddy Super Bill Bradley has fond memories of those days they spent as teammates in Philadelphia.

"Billy is my old roommate," Bradley said. "The flash from prep school who went to Villanova. He was a very smart player who was so fast he could run a hole in the wind. He had great hands. Billy was a pleasant guy who had a great sense of humor."

Tim Rossovich had similar recollections of his old friend.

"Billy and Bill Bradley and I were very close friends," he said. "He never got the credit he deserved. Billy went 100 percent all the time. That's why I have so much respect for him."

While the Eagles had little success on the field, Walik appreciated the opportunity to play in Philadelphia. That appreciation only increased when he moved on to Winnipeg in the Canadian Football League and Florida of the World Football League.

"My passion for football left after I left the Eagles," Bill Walik said. "I loved Philadelphia. They made you feel like part of the community. Of course, I didn't fumble the ball or throw it away much. The community really embraced me. Being in Philadelphia was a nice transition away from young adulthood into the real world."

Since his career ended, the real world for Bill Walik has been in Bainbridge Island, Washington, a short ferry ride from Seattle, where he has been employed as a municipal bond trader.

"We came out here about thirty years ago, in 1975," he said. "It's a great place to live. I've been involved trading municipal bonds, working in the investment securities industries. You go from one firm to the next."

It's hard to believe that Billy Walik, the kid from Villanova, is now sixty-seven years old. Time passes faster than we ever realize.

"When you play sports or have a passion for sports, you are like a little kid in many ways," he said. "Time can stand still."

Chapter Four

THE KICKERS

Where Have You Gone?

HAPPY FELLER

When the Eagles drafted James "Happy" Feller in the fourth round of the 1971 draft out of Texas, he brought a pedigree of winning. Thanks in no small part to his powerful right leg, the Longhornes won 30 straight games and two national titles during his tenure there. Could there be any doubt that similar success would follow Feller into the pros?

Feller, who got his nickname when he was a baby who laughed quite often, had a very strong training camp with the Eagles. He beat out incumbent kicker Mark Moseley, who went on to a number of successful seasons with the Washington Redskins. But Feller was happy with the Eagles and really enjoyed Philadelphia.

"I loved Philadelphia," he said. "It's a great city. I don't think that I ever lived in a place that I enjoyed more. The people were just great. I still go up there every couple of years and go to South Street and go to Jim's Steaks.

"I didn't really think that there would be that much of an adjustment from college to the pros. The only adjustment that I had to make was going from an atmosphere in Texas that was lively and emotional to Philadelphia where it was more like a business."

The Eagles were a losing football team and Happy Feller began having some problems during his rookie season. By year's end, he converted

Photo courtesy of the Philadelphia Eagles

#1 · HAPPY FELLER
University of Texas • Hgt: 6-1 • Wgt: 185

Position: Place Kicker
Three-Year NFL Career
Eagles One Year (1971)

on just six of 20 field goal attempts. Unlike in his college career, Feller was struggling with the Birds.

"I wish I had the maturity then that I do now," Feller said. "At training camp of my rookie year, I kicked really well and beat out Mark Moseley. As soon as I made the team, early in the season, Jerry Williams was fired as coach by the owner of the team, Leonard Tose. Ed Khayat who had been at New Orleans was promoted to interim head coach. Khayat brought in Tom Dempsey who had been cut by the Saints as a taxi squad person. When I saw that, I knew he ultimately would go with Dempsey. I began to question my ability. I should have never lost my belief in myself. Looking back, I wished I had the mental maturity. My whole attitude toward the head coach and the team changed."

Feller continued to struggle, but he felt he was treated fairly by the fans, who have a reputation of being very tough in the NFL.

"They were known as the boo birds," he said. "But I think they were justified in booing. My rookie year we only won two or three games. So the team was not the best in the world. But one on one, when you talk to the fans, they're very friendly."

Feller moved on to the Saints where he kicked for the next two seasons, but a quadricep injury then slowed his progress, and his career ended after three disappointing NFL seasons.

"Any time anybody doesn't reach their potential and falls short of their own expectations, you look back and wonder," he said. "I just wish I had the maturity at 21 that I do now . . . When you have a dream and don't fully realize it, there is remorse that you didn't do better.

"But I made some wonderful friends. Players, good and bad, have a tremendous amount of empathy for each other, because it will only last for a short time and it's tough and demanding. The fans see the superstars. But the average guy lasts only three or four years. So there is a lot of empathy and camaraderie, a real love for each other."

Following his short NFL career, Happy Feller went to work for the Bell System for more than seven years before forming his own company, Teledynamics, in 1981. He hopes to be remembered for his successes as well as for the person he is.

"I guess I'd like to be remembered for the skill as a kicker I had at the University of Texas," Feller said. "My kicking as a pro never fully exemplified my ability, which was a psychological stumble on my part. But also, I'd like to be thought of as just a good guy. Someone who was compassionate, understanding and kind."

Where Have You Gone?

TONY FRANKLIN

B roadway Joe Namath had his signature white shoes. Big Ben Davidson had that imposing handlebar mustache. And former Eagles, Patriots and Dolphins kicker Tony Franklin had that bare right foot.

The Eagles made Franklin their third choice in the 1979 draft after a horrendous playoff experience the previous season. Franklin had a strong leg and nerves of steel. All prerequisites for playing in Philadelphia, particularly as a kicker.

"I knew nothing whatsoever of Philadelphia, so it was quite a culture shock for a kid to basically come out of Texas for the first time," Tony Franklin said. "I've been cheered there and I've been booed there. They have very knowledgeable fans who can recognize a guy who is going all out or dogging it. I like the fans there. When you have a great game, they cheer you. When you play a horrible game, they let you know about it. Dealing with that is part of being a professional. But my wife and I still love the city of Philadelphia."

For the most part, the city loved him back.

During his rookie season, Franklin hit on 23 of 31 field goal attempts, earning second-team All-NFC honors from UPI. He booted a 46-yard field goal in his first regular-season game, a 23-17 win over the hated New York Giants and kicked four field goals in a 26-14 victory at

Photo courtesy of the Philadelphia Eagles

#1 · TONY FRANKLIN
Texas A & M • Hgt: 5-8 • Wgt: 182 • Born: November 18, 1956

Position: Kicker
10-Year NFL Career
Eagles Five Years (1979-1983)

New Orleans. Then he set a team record with an amazing 59-yard field goal at Dallas on *Monday Night Football.*

However, he got in Coach Dick Vermeil's doghouse thanks to a kickoff in the postseason of his first year, when he disobeyed the coach's order to kick deep late in the loss at Tampa Bay. He tried an onside kick that failed, bringing the coach's wrath upon him. In spite of an outstanding rookie season, Vermeil openly questioned Franklin's maturity.

"Our relationship was stressed at times," Franklin said of his times with Dick Vermeil. "Dick has mellowed out over the years and so have I. Some of the stuff he got on me about I understand, I was a headstrong kid. We clashed sometimes. But I also liked Dick personally. I was glad he won his first Super Bowl and he's doing a fine job in Kansas City. He is loyal to the end."

Franklin kicked a total of 80 field goals out of 128 attempts (62.5 percent) and 172 extra points for the Birds. Not bad for a guy with only one shoe.

"I never could kick with a shoe on," he said of his signature barefoot kicking style. "Wearing a shoe I was not as accurate and could not kick it as far. I worked on it in high school and still have the school record with a 58-yard field goal. I just kicked it better that way."

If opposing players tried to injure his bare kicking foot, Franklin was unaware of any such efforts.

"If they did, I wasn't aware of it," he said. "Nobody ever went out of their way to stomp on my foot. They'd go after me and blow me up on coverage, but that's just their job. But it's not like anyone went after my feet."

He played for the Eagles through the 1983 season, after which he was traded to New England for a sixth-round draft pick. While with the Patriots, his career blossomed and Franklin had a Pro Bowl season for the Patriots in 1986. He finished up with Miami in 1988.

"I was very fortunate and blessed to be able to play," he said. "I was one of 28 guys out of about 125 million men who got paid for playing a kid's game. My career meant a lot to me. My kids, my wife, my entire family are very proud of me. It all means more to me as I get older.

"I've also been able to make a lot of business connections and really enjoy what I'm doing."

Tony Franklin has been in charge of finance for a large Honda and Mitsubishi dealer in San Antonio, Ramsay Gillman. He has also been involved in broadcasting high school football.

Franklin hopes that his efforts will be remembered and appreciated.

"I was a guy who went out and tried his best," he said. "One of the best things that happened to me was getting traded to New England. It was a fresh start for me. I was a guy who tried his best and was well prepared on Sunday. I love the game and have great memories of Philadelphia. It's a great sports town and I made some good friends up there."

MARK MOSELEY

For the last five years of his National Football League career, Mark Moseley was the last of the straight-on kickers, quite possibly the final non-soccer-style place kicker the game will see. He helped the Washington Redskins to a Super Bowl title and was voted the league's Most Valuable Player in 1982, the first kicker to be so honored in the history of the league. He was known for having icewater in his veins with numerous last-second, game-winning field goals.

But what many fans don't realize is that Mark Moseley was once a Philadelphia Eagle. Drafted by the Birds out of Stephen F. Austin State College in Texas, Moseley beat out veteran Sam Baker to be the Eagles place kicker in 1970. His rookie training camp was not filled with warmth from his key kicking competitor.

"When I got to Philly I didn't realize that I had to make the team," Moseley said. "I thought I was assured of making the team. Sam Baker didn't say a word to me the whole training camp. When he got cut at the end of camp, he left a green kicking shoe with a lead weight in my locker with a note wishing me luck."

It wasn't a great season for the strong-legged kicker as he hit on 14 of 25 field goal attempts and 25 of 28 extra points. As the year wore on he developed a sore leg as he was thrown into punting duties after Bill Bradley suffered a knee injury.

AP/WWP

#3 · MARK MOSELEY
Stephen F. Austin State • Hgt: 6-0 • Wgt: 185 • Born: March 12, 1948

Position: Kicker
16-Year NFL Career
Eagles One Year (1970)

While trying to adjust to life in the NFL, Mark Moseley gained an appreciation for Philadelphia.

"It wasn't a stellar year for me," he said. "About halfway through the year I kicked my leg out. I didn't know much about the city, which was still an older kind of town in those days. I was really impressed with the Philadelphia subways, the hoagies. They were the best. One time I took one all the way to Texas with me on a plane."

Before the following year, the Eagles drafted a great Texas Longhorne kicker named James Happy Feller in the fourth round of the draft. Even though Moseley thought he outkicked Feller, he was less than a happy guy after being cut by the Eagles.

"It was terribly disappointing because I had worked hard to get myself in physical shape," Moseley said. "I was scared to death my entire rookie year. In my second year I was ready to let it go. I've always been a pretty confident person with my ability to kick a football."

After a brief stint in Houston and nearly two years out of football, Redskins Coach George Allen called on Moseley to come to Washington. It was his 13 seasons spent in the nation's capital that will probably see Moseley enshrined in the Hall of Fame in Canton, Ohio.

"It was great being in a historic football city like Washington where the Redskins are legendary," he said. "It was a pleasure to be there under George Allen. He gave me a chance to revitalize my career. I competed against 12 kickers to win the job. I was very fortunate. When I got to Washington, I was not going to let it get away from me."

Moseley led the 'Skins in scoring from 1974 to 1985 and was a four-time All-Pro selection. His 300 career field goals place him fifth on the all-time list. He enjoyed his short time in Philadelphia and gives Eagles fans some credit for his later successes.

"They have good fans there," he said. "They're rowdy fans, but they support their team. When I think of Philadelphia fans, I think of good, hard-working, blue-collar fans who love their Eagles. It takes a special person to play there. They got on me a little bit, and those early days made me tougher as I got older. They taught me to be tough. That helped me become such a good last-second kicker.

"I've always felt fondness toward Philly fans. They got me started, and I appreciated that."

While Mark Moseley certainly has the credentials for Hall of Fame consideration, he prefers to be thought of as someone who was a football player, ready to compete each and every week.

"I'd like to be remembered as a guy who played as hard as he could and left it all on the field," he said. "I always prided myself on working hard during the week to be prepared for every game. I left it all on the field and gave it everything I had."

Following his playing days, Moseley was in business for 16 years in the travel industry, commercial real estate and motivational speaking. He is now the director of franchise development for Five Guys Burgers And Fries, a burger and fries restaurant chain.

He and his wife, Sandy, have nine children and thirteen grandchildren.

Chapter Five

THE "O" LINE

ED BLAINE

W hatever happened to Ed Blaine? That question was asked often in the mid-1960s as Blaine, an outstanding young offensive lineman, seemingly disappeared off the face of the Earth. A second-round pick of the Green Bay Packers in the 1962 draft out of Missouri, the former All-American and All-Big Eight player backed up a couple of talented Packer guards in Jerry Kramer and Fuzzy Thurston.

After being sent to the Birds toward the end of training camp in 1963, he immediately became a starter who played in 56 games for Philadelphia. Known as an outstanding pulling guard and an excellent blocker, Blaine seemed on the fast track to becoming an All-Pro performer who could have had a long career.

But Ed Blaine is a man of honor, and a promise that he had made to a college professor led him to give up the game and return to his education, which has in turn led to an extraordinary career in science.

"When I was playing for Missouri, I was a lightweight lineman," he said. "A lot of people told me that I was too light to play pro football. But I felt like I had to play in the NFL, being such a high draft choice.

"I had promised one of my professors, Clint Conawa, that I'd only play for five years and then retire and finish my PhD and go into science. I had a great opportunity to participate in one of the things that many people can't do in playing football. But I found something I liked

Photo courtesy of the Philadelphia Eagles

#64 · ED BLAINE
Missouri • Hgt: 6-2 • Wgt: 235 • Born: January 30, 1940

Position: Guard
Five-Year NFL Career
Eagles Four Years (1963-1966)

equally as well. I could have played longer, maybe ten years, but I never could have had the career I've had as a scientist."

Teamed with some outstanding linemen such as Bob Brown, Jim Skaggs and Jim Ringo, Blaine earned First-Team All-Eastern Conference honors from *The Sporting News* in 1964. After informing the Eagles of his decision not to return following the 1966 season, the team felt he was simply trying to get more money. But that was not the case.

"I love Philadelphia," he said. "It's one of my favorite places. I spent about ten years in the area in my post-football career at Merck. Philadelphia is just a nice city. I like the feel of it. It's like a big city, but not like New York.

"When I retired, a lot of people were unhappy and accused me of turning my back on them. But I had made a promise to this person and had to honor it. I did, and it's worked out very well. I loved football. I still do. When I played football I had six months to bang people around. Then I'd go back to the University for six months in a more intellectual environment. It was a good balance and a wonderful time in my life for five years.

"Was it the right choice? Had my scientific career been less successful, I would have had more doubts and second thoughts. But the reality of it is that I've accepted the decision. It was the right one."

Blaine obtained his PhD in physiology from the University of Missouri and did his postdoctoral work at the Howard Florey Institute for Experimental Physiology and Medicine at the University of Melbourne.

He has worked in such areas as investigating renal excretory function and blood pressure regulation. Currently, he is involved in the study of fluid balance and cardiovascular function with emphasis on hypertension and heart failure in Missouri. Ed Blaine has gone from creating holes for running backs and protecting quarterbacks to the basic science of trying to find out what causes diseases and discovering cures for them.

Giving up professional football was a tough decision to make, but nearly 50 years after the fact, it seems certain that Ed Blaine made the correct choice.

"When you have to make a tough decision, you have to go with your heart," he said. "Do what you really feel compelled to do. You have to live honorably, and keeping my promise was important. It all worked out."

That being said, Blaine also takes pride in his gridiron career.

"I hope to be thought of as a good, solid player who represented Philadelphia well," he said. "I loved the city and gave the game 100 percent. I always did my best and was reasonably successful."

LANE HOWELL

W hen Lane Howell came to the Eagles from the New York Giants in 1965 in exchange for Pete Case, he became part of one of the best offensive lines in football. Win or lose, there was no denying the talent on that O-line with the likes of Howell, Bob Brown, Jim Ringo, Jim Skaggs and Ed Blaine.

Drafted by the Giants out of college, Howell gained experience in New York before coming to Philadelphia. No matter where Lane Howell played, he was thrilled to be a player in the National Football League.

"The feeling you have being a player in the NFL is a special thrill," he said. "It doesn't matter where you play, all of the teams in the NFL have quality teams with quality people. The feeling that I had being an NFL player was number one. In New York, I didn't know much about Philadelphia except the fact that we played them every year, and that it was a pretty good team.

"We always had a good offense with the Eagles. Every year we had some scorers. It was a very productive offense. I give our offensive coach, Dick Stanfield, a lot of credit. Once you have a guy like Bob Brown, who is in the football Hall of Fame, you are off to a pretty good start."

During his tenure in Philadelphia, there weren't many good starts as the team suffered through losing seasons despite having some talented

AP/WWP

#79 · Lane Howell
Grambling • Hgt: 6-5 • Wgt: 270 • Born: July 28, 1941

Position: Offensive Tackle
Seven-Year NFL Career
Eagles Five Years (1965-1969)

players on the team. Lane Howell wanted to win and did his best to help make that happen.

"You are a professional and you always feel like you can win," he said. "The difference in the ability of the players in the NFL is minute. The successful teams seem to get a group together that has chemistry.

"You play because you love the game. At the time we were losing in Philadelphia, you almost expected something terrible to happen. You'd be playing well and then some fluke happens and you lose. So you play for yourself, for your pride. You are not going to be embarrassed out there."

Philadelphia Eagles fans have a reputation around the league for being very demanding and unforgiving. There were times during his career when Howell felt their wrath.

"I think they were very knowledgeable of the game," he said. "They were very vocal. But it seemed like if they got the boos out for you that it was very hard to turn that around. After that you could never do anything to meet their expectations. It's like they held a grudge. I can still hear them now when I see a game on TV."

Remembered as a great teammate, Howell's efforts were appreciated in the huddle and on the sidelines.

"He was a real team player," said former teammate Leroy Keyes. "One time when we were playing the Rams, I knocked Deacon Jones down with a hard block and then stood over him. Jones told me he was going to get me. It was only the first quarter of the game so he had plenty of time left. But Lane came over to me and told me that he had my back. I really appreciated that.

"He was a good team player. He was a big man who really understood the game. He got caught holding a couple of times and the fans needed somebody to be the scapegoat. But what a great guy."

Howell played with the Birds through the 1969 season and retired from the game. He was employed by ARA Services and JB Lippencott Publishing before returned home to Monroe Louisiana, where he taught junior high school for four years. In 1992, Howell returned to his alma mater, Grambling, as athletic compliance officer. Coming full circle has been a pleasant experience for No. 79.

"It's been a blessing to come full circle like this," he said. "At this point in my life I can't think of anywhere I'd rather be. I'm a simple person. I like to fish, work in the garden, my church activities. Being home at this time is wonderful."

WADE KEY

L ike many athletes who come from the south, Wade Key not only had to make the adjustments necessary to make the Philadelphia Eagles roster as a 13th-round draft pick, but he also had some major changes to make living in the northeast part of the country. It was a totally different world from his native Texas.

"In the beginning I really felt like a duck out of water being from Texas," Key said. "You go up there to Philadelphia and you see how people are different. I was not accustomed to it. It was totally the unknown to me. You have no inclination of how different an environment it is.

"It was very enjoyable. I'm 57 years old now, closing in on 58 and looking back, it really was the best time of my life. I learned to love the people in South Philadelphia in all the mom and pop pizza places and restaurants. It was so much fun. By the time I left, I felt as if it was the best time in my life."

Wade Key was a solid, if not spectacular offensive lineman for some bad Eagles teams as well as some pretty good Philadelphia teams. But regardless of how many wins the team had during a particular season, he was a steady performer. Coming from a very successful college program at South West Texas State, losing seasons were tough to take.

"There were some long, long seasons," Key said. "I never liked losing. In college in 1967, we were the number-one NAI team in the

Photo courtesy of the Philadelphia Eagles

#72 · WADE KEY
South Western Texas State • Hgt: 6-5 • Wgt: 260
Born: October 14, 1946

Position: Guard / Tackle
11-Year NFL Career
Eagles 11 Years (1970-1980)

country. At that point of my life I had stars in my eyes. I was just married and out of college and ready to challenge the world. When you lose you have to keep pressing on. You don't like it, but you continue on and try to get better."

Improvement for the Eagles of his generation was slow, to be sure. Part of the frustration over so many losing teams was the realization that there were plenty of talented football players in Philadelphia. Key looks upon those days, the fans and his teammates with high regard.

"We had some great football players on those teams," he said. "There were guys like Tim Rossovich, Ron Jaworski, Wilbert Montgomery, Jerry Sizemore, Guy Morriss, Steve Kinney and Mel Tom. There were some good coaches there also. Sometimes the chemistry is not right. That was the problem until Dick Vermeil arrived. He turned it all around. Dick was a hard man to play for. He was a demanding guy with long practices.

"I think the fans were like me. They hated to lose and they expressed themselves very well. And I do the same thing. Winning becomes what you are and who you are. When you don't achieve that, it's a stressful time."

Toward the end of Wade Key's playing career, he did enjoy winning seasons at the beginning of the Vermeil era. After his playing days ended, he worked in farming, ranching and construction for a while. But all of his experience as a professional football player trained him well for his career as a high school football coach in his native Texas for 22 years before retiring. He was also the offensive coordinator for Sam Houston High School in San Antonio.

"High school football is very serious business," he said. "If you look at some of the top programs in the country like Nebraska, Oklahoma, and other major colleges, you'll see a lot of Texas kids there. The Eagles always had a lot of players from Texas.

"In the high school business, we are teaching life skills. What you learn about in athletics will apply to most every situation in life. I learned a lot of life skills, had fun and some God-given talents and wanted to give back to the game through coaching."

Wade Key may not have been a star, but he was one of the steadiest lineman to ever grace the Eagles team. He hopes to be remembered as someone who showed up through thick and thin.

"I think my forte as a player was being steady," he said. "I wasn't an All-Pro or a superstar. But I lined up and played a whole lot of days. I lined up and was one of the guys who did the best he could do for the Philadelphia Eagles."

GUY MORRISS

I f you ever need an example of a solid football player who did an outstanding job each and every week while being a quiet leader on the team, look no further than Guy Morriss. The majority of his 15-year NFL playing career was spent with the Eagles, where he more than lived up to his potential as a second-round draft pick in 1973.

He was an All-Pro who appeared in two Super Bowls, with the Eagles in 1981 and the Patriots in 1985.

When Guy Morriss came to Philadelphia, he arrived with great credentials as an All-Southwest Conference lineman at TCU. But the Texas native had a tough time with the adjustment at his first training camp with the Eagles. Another Texas native, defensive back Bill Bradley, went out of his way to help Morriss out.

"I was three weeks late to camp because of the college All-Star Games," Morriss recalled. "So I was late and wasn't playing very good to start with. I was really struggling and behind and homesick. But Bill Bradley probably saved my career. He took me under his wing and kept me from going home."

Thanks to Super Bill, Morriss stuck it out and became one of the best offensive linemen in the game. And he also developed a real appreciation for the city of Philadelphia and Eagles fans.

AP/WWP

#50 · GUY MORRISS
TCU • Hgt: 6-4 • Wgt: 240 • Born: May 13, 1951

Position: Center
15-Year NFL Career
Eagles 11 years (1973-1983)

"I fell in love with the city, and the city fell in love with me," he said. "I rented a house off of Packer Avenue and the whole community adopted me and my family. I was overwhelmed by the city of Philadelphia. They have really good fans who are appreciative when you do good.

"They pay good money to see you perform. When you do good, they let you know. And they also let you know when you do bad. That's fair, it's the nature of the beast. I just fell in love with those fans."

The fortunes of the Birds began to improve with the hiring of young Dick Vermeil from UCLA as coach. The Eagles improved each year and joined the Phillies, Flyers and Sixers as winning franchises in the late 1970s. It was Vermeil who steered the ship to the ultimate pro football game, the Super Bowl, by surrounding himself with players who mirrored his work ethic.

"When I think of Dick Vermeil, I think of his work ethic more than anything else," he said. "He was relentless in his approach and preparation for a game. At times it was hard on the players, because he would always second-guess himself on our game plan and kept changing it during the week. He always tried to come up with the perfect plan. But he did it for all the right reasons. He always preached that if we hang onto the rope after everyone else lets go, that we would win a lot of games in the fourth quarter. And we did."

When the Eagles reached the Super Bowl in 1981 against the Oakland Raiders, they were a confident team that most people expected to win. But the Super Bowl was not the Eagles' day. The reasons for the disappointing defeat are still up for debate.

"I think what hurt us that day is that we were a tired football team on game day," said Morriss. "That was the youth and energy in Dick Vermeil coming out. We left something on the practice field. We felt good about the game because we had beaten Oakland earlier that season. But they got three days to relax on Bourbon Street in New Orleans and we took the opposite approach.

"It really hurt, but I got over it. It was very disappointing."

After leaving the Eagles, Morriss played with the New England Patriots for four seasons, with another disappointing Super Bowl appearance against the Chicago Bears. He began a long and successful coaching career in 1988 that has taken him to numerous cities as a college and professional coach. But his stock as a player was very high as he was respected for his ability and drive.

"It all starts in the middle of the offensive line," said former teammate Jerry Sizemore. "He was a wonderful guy, kind of a wild guy.

We were roommates, old partners from Texas. He was a tremendous competitor who did a great job."

In 2003, he left his position as head coach at Kentucky to take the same position with Baylor University. The Vermeil work ethic has followed Guy Morriss throughout his coaching career.

"That's how we coach here at Baylor," he said. "We don't out-scheme anybody, we outwork them. Schemes don't win football games. It's not meant to be pretty or flashy. I believe in old-fashioned hard work and fundamentals. I think a lot of coaches miss the boat that way. It's hard work, there is no magic formula."

Morriss coached Baylor for five seasons with an 18-40 record. After appending a year as a position coach at Kentucky State University, he became head coach at Texas A&M–Commerce. Following four seasons with a 10-31 record from 2009 through 2012, he now serves as Special Assistant to the Athletic Director.

The lifelong love affair that Guy Morriss has had with football continues to this day. "I miss playing to this very day," he said. "My body clock starts ticking every July. All I've ever done is play and coach football. And I'd still be playing if my body would let me.

"I've always tried to be a good person who gave something back to the community. I'm just an average, normal guy and an old-fashioned hard worker. I had fun in Philadelphia with the Eagles. It was a great time in my life. I love it. It's a great city."

JERRY SIZEMORE

M uch like songstress Judy Collins, former Philadelphia Eagles
tackle Jerry Sizemore has looked at football from both sides. As a
young player, a first-round draft pick out of Texas and the third overall
pick in 1973, he had more than his fair share of losing. But then under
Coach Dick Vermeil, he also enjoyed five consecutive playoff seasons
from 1978 to '82.

During his career, Sizemore started 127 consecutive games and
helped anchor a strong offensive line that helped lead the Eagles to the
NFC Championship in 1980 and a berth in Super Bowl XV. He is a
member of the College Hall of Fame and a proud inductee of the Eagles
Honor Roll. But back in 1973, he didn't know much about the city of
Philadelphia.

"Well, you read a lot about the city in the history books," Sizemore
said. "Fortunately, a good friend of mine, Bill Bradley, was there with
the Eagles. We also had a kicker from Texas who played there, Happy
Feller. So I know a little bit about Philadelphia. I was excited to be
drafted so early, got involved with Mike McCormick who was the head
coach. Philadelphia was a wonderful place to play, a real blessing.

"Bill Bradley showed me around. He and I were roommates my first
year at the Ben Franklin Hotel. I'll never forget, we paid $285 a person
a month. The more I got out and around, I discovered that Philadelphia

Photo courtesy of the Philadelphia Eagles

#76 · JERRY SIZEMORE
Texas • Hgt: 6-4 • Wgt: 265 • Born: July 16, 1951

Position: Offensive Lineman
12-Year NFL Career
Eagles 12 years (1973-1984)

was a wonderful place. The people were so sincere. Everybody took care of each other. I really enjoyed it. A large part of my heart is still in Philly. It you give it a good effort, they're behind you. I knew that if we could ever turn it around that Philly would be a great place to play."

And turn it around they did. Under Dick Vermeil, they worked harder than they had ever worked. But they also began to win and succeed.

"We got no respect early on," Sizemore said. "We had to earn every drop of sweat at a time. We went from being one of the worst teams in the league to the Super Bowl.

"I think about Dick Vermeil all the time, bless his soul. It was incredible the way he treated people. He was a wonderful motivator. He worked us really hard, but there is not a finer coach in the business. We got better and better. He studied the game and had a great way of judging character in people."

The Eagles' Super Bowl experience was not a good one. There are as many theories about why the team came out so flat that Sunday as there are people in the city of Philadelphia. But there is little doubt that the NFC Championship victory over Dallas was a hard act to follow. And a two-week rest before Super Bowl XV made it tough to focus on the task at hand.

"In order to get to the Super Bowl, we had to play Dallas in Philadelphia to advance," Sizemore said. "We didn't know anything about Super Bowl week. I think we got ready too early. We came out flat as a pancake. I know when I got on the field I could hardly breathe. We got to the stadium like six hours before the game and watched the hostages being released on television. Oakland came out all loosey-goosey. For us it was a real team effort. Nobody had a good game.

"It was a wonderful ride getting to that game, going from the worst to the best in five years. But we lost and we lost badly. We were never in the game. I just felt so low. I was the last one out of the locker room. It was a deflating, demoralizing feeling. I never felt that bad. Second place in the Super Bowl is not what you think it would be.

"I didn't play well. It was all a nightmare. But getting there was probably the highlight of my career."

Sizemore played through the 1984 season and now spends time in his home on Lake Travis in Lago Vista, Texas with his family. He owns a boat stop called Rock Marina and also works in real estate.

He misses Philadelphia and playing the game he enjoyed for so many years. And he is very proud of his accomplishments and fond of the many people who touched his life.

"I was very blessed," Sizemore said. "I was at the right place at the right time. Being drafted by Philly could not have been better. I was more into the team than I was individual things. One of the most frustrating things is that I don't know if I let everyone know how much I appreciated them. From my teammates to the people who worked at the Vet, to the folks who owned the hoagie shops to all of the fans. I really appreciated them and miss them. There is a terrible void."

Life had been good for Jerry Sizemore. As far as he is concerned, that is true in no small part because of his time in Philadelphia as a member of the Eagles.

JIM SKAGGS

E ven though the Eagles teams of the mid-to-late 1960s lost more than they won, it wasn't due to a lack of talent. The offensive line had some premier players like Jim Ringo, Lane Howell, Bob Brown, Ed Blaine and Jim Skaggs. Chosen in the 10th round of the 1962 draft, Skaggs spurned an offer from the American Football League's Oakland Raiders to sign with the Eagles.

"In those days, the old AFL was sort of a minor league," Skaggs said from his home in Washington. "This was before they got involved in the wage wars. Most of the guys who could go and play in the NFL did so. That changed when the AFL owners got really competitive and started drafting and signing some really good players, which of course, expedited the merger."

You couldn't blame a young player who signed with Philadelphia to expect success with the team. After all, the Birds won the NFL Championship in 1960 and were runners up the following year. Little did Jim Skaggs know when he joined the team in 1962 that he would enjoy only one winning season, 1966, in his entire 11-year career. Quite a difference from his college days at Washington where the Huskies played in two Rose Bowls.

"Well, in the early years they had just won what they called the world championship two years before I got there," he said. "But for the

Courtesy of the Philadelphia Eagles

#70 · JIM SKAGGS
Washington • Hgt: 6-2 • Wgt: 255 • Born: January 3, 1940

Position: Offensive Lineman
11-Year NFL Career
Eagles 11 years (1962-1972)

time I was there we had not a very good record. It was frustrating not being more competitive. It wore on you. A lot of times I felt we should do better. But I made some good friends there, people I'll never forget. And the losing didn't completely take away from the joy and fun that we had lining up against some of the great players of the day like Alex Karras and Merlin Olson. I just loved when Sunday came."

Skaggs was a popular player in the locker room where his teammates appreciated his work ethic and dedication to the team.

"He was just an ironhorse of a guy who worked his butt off," said defensive back Bill Bradley. "Jim was a very intelligent offensive lineman and a model citizen."

Skaggs was responsible, among other things, for protecting the quarterback on passing plays. His efforts were greatly appreciated by the signal callers.

"He was the best football player I ever played with," said Norm Snead. "Jim was the strongest man I ever knew. He should be in the Hall of Fame. I never had to worry about anyone he played against."

A native of California, Skaggs and his wife always returned to Washington state in the off season. But he knew the Delaware Valley well and really enjoyed the fans, boo-birds or not.

"It was such a fun time in my life, I really enjoyed it," he said. "I thought the fans were great. They booed, but they had some reason to boo. But they were always gracious to me and they had lots of fun in the stands.

"We didn't stay in the off season, always returning to the northwest. We lived all around the area in New Jersey, Philadelphia and the area surrounding Philadelphia. I have no regrets at all. I spent my whole career in Philadelphia, which is not the case all that often. I felt fortunate to be able to be there. It was a real fulfilling part of my life."

Jim Skaggs decided to retire from the game following the 1972 season, feeling that he had played as long as he could have. A new coaching staff with Mike McCormick at the helm promised widespread changes, and it seemed like a good time to go out still on top of his game.

"He was a warrior," said former funning back and free safety Leroy Keyes. "He was a pro who was a gamer and a fighter."

Skaggs got involved in the insurance industry and enjoyed a long career with State Farm Insurance, first as an agent then in management. After a successful 29-year tenure, he is now happily retired and enjoying the fruits of his labor.

"I'd hope that people would remember me as a pretty good lineman that always tried his best and enjoyed what he did," Skaggs said. "You see a lot of troublemakers today and involvement with drugs. It's frustrating to see kids getting into that kind of stuff now. I never got involved with any of that. I guess I was pretty much a straight arrow."

Chapter Six

THE CONCRETE WALL

CHUCK
BEDNARIK

"Concrete Charley" Bednarik was the Philadelphia Eagles. No single player epitomized a franchise or team more than old No. 60, and no new regime can erase the impact the man had on the game, as well as the franchise.

The last of the two-way players, Bednarik was an ironman who played both on offense and defense. In fact, in the National Football League Championship game in front of 67,000 fans at Franklin Field on December 26, 1960 against the Green Bay Packers, he played in 135 of the games 138 plays.

It was the only postseason game that Packers Coach Vince Lombardi ever lost. And it was Bednarik who saved the game for the Birds by making a crunching, open-field tackle on Jimmie Taylor inside the Eagles' 10-yard line in the closing seconds of the game to cinch the 17-13 victory.

Elected to the pro football Hall of Fame in 1967, he was the MVP of the 1954 Pro Bowl, one of his team-record eight Pro Bowl appearances. He was named to the Eagles All-Time Team and was cited as Lineman of the Decade for the 1950s. Coming out of the University of Pennsylvania, Bednarik was the first offensive lineman to win the Maxwell Award and finished third in voting for the Heisman Trophy.

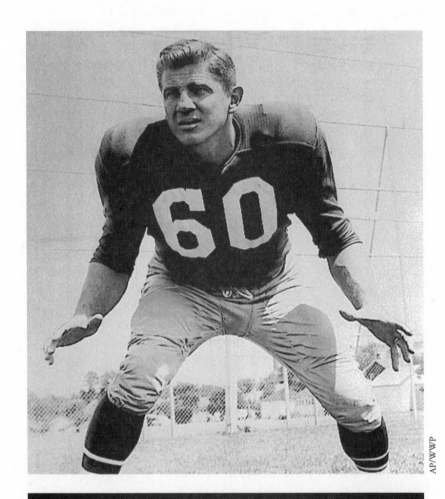

AP/WWP

#60 · CHUCK BEDNARIK
University of Pennsylvania • Hgt: 6-3 • Wgt: 240 • Born: May 1, 1925
Died: March 21, 2015

Position: Center / Linebacker
14-Year NFL Career
Eagles 14 Years (1949-1962)

No name is more synonymous with the Philadelphia Eagles than Chuck Bednarik. Even though the times have created a different brand of football, he is the measuring stick of true greatness.

"The game has changed drastically over the years," he said at the turn of the century. "It's all specialization now. To people born later, they accept it because it's all they've ever known. But the game of football isn't what it was originated to be. It's a different game altogether now. Football was an ironman's game. Now they're overpaid and underplayed. These guys are pussycats for the little time they put on the field. I haven't been to a game in years. A guy has to come into the game just to hold the ball for extra points and field goals? I'm 79 years old, and I could snap the ball for a punt or field goal now.

"When I played, not one guy on the team weighed 300 pounds. Now you've got guys coming in at 350 and 360 pounds. They're just trying to suck in air now. It would be impossible for them to play two ways. They are a bunch of overweight, fat pigs."

After serving in the military in World War II, Bednarik, a native of Bethlehem Pennsylvania, attended college at the University of Pennsylvania. He came to the Eagles as a bonus pick in the 1949 draft in the first round. After missing his first two games in his rookie season with pneumonia, he missed just one game in the next 14 years.

Playing on both sides of the line provided Bednarik with the opportunity to excel and dominate games. But he did prefer playing defense over offense.

"As a center you snap the ball to the quarterback and then do your job," he said. "Who watches the center? Nobody sees us. I'd much rather play defense and kick the shit out of some guy. You can stand out on every play."

The 1960 world championship team represents the highlight of Bednarik's career. His guarantee of an Eagles victory to the fans beat New York Jets quarterback Joe Namath's boast by nine years. As far as Concrete Charley is concerned, it was the addition of Norm Van Brocklin that sealed the deal for the Eagles.

"It was a real pleasure to see us get Norm Van Brocklin from the Los Angeles Rams," he said.

"How the quarterback goes, the team goes. He was our leader."

When Bednarik hit a player, it felt like being hit by concrete. But he got the Concrete Charley nickname from his job with Warner Concrete, where he was employed in the off season as a concrete salesman.

Of his many accomplishments in his Hall of Fame career, Chuck Bednarik's most famous moment is probably his hit on New York

Giants running back Frank Gifford, which put Giff out of football for an entire year. It was a clean hit, but a Concrete Charley hit.

"If you're going to do anything big, do it in New York," he said. "The game just happened to be in New York, and if it would have been just an ordinary running back, the whole thing would have been forgotten. But thanks to it being Frank Gifford, number one, and in New York, number two, and the New York press, people knew all about it."

Following the end of his illustrious career in 1962, Bednarik worked in sales. He served as Chairman of the Pennsylvania State Athletic Commission in charge of boxing. He had been appointed by six different governors.

Although for the most part estranged from the Eagles organization, he hoped his impact as a player and person would be remembered and appreciated.

"I was a two-way player who made contact on every play on offense and defense," he said. "A concrete player on every play. I was always a decent person who never did anything bad or nasty to anyone. I was the last of the two-way players."

Chuck Bednarik, the last of the iron men in football, passed away on March 21, 2015. The Philadelphia Eagles said, in a statement, that he died after a brief illness. But Bednarik's daughter, Charlene, stated that he suffered from Alzheimer's Disease and had suffered from dementia for years. Regardless, Chuck Bednarik was one of a kind. Chuck Bednarik was the Philadelphia Eagles.

Chapter Seven

THE MINISTER OF DEFENSE

Where Have You Gone?

REGGIE WHITE

Reginald Howard "Reggie" White may simply have been the best defensive player in the history of the National Football League. The way he played and acted on and off the football field was the stuff of legend. He was so much more than a football player. But to understand his value on the field, a statistical look at his career is necessary and awe-inspiring.

He was an All-Pro selection in 13 of his 15 seasons in the NFL, named to the First Team 10 times and was Pro Bowl MVP once. This Super Bowl champion with Green Bay also was a two-time NFL Defensive Player of the Year, a two-time NFL sacks leader and still holds the NFL record with at least 9 sacks in 10 consecutive seasons.

White was voted to the NFL 75th Anniversary All-Time team, was named to the 1980's All-Decade team, the 1990's All-Decade team and has had his number 92 retired by his alma mater, the Tennessee Volunteers, the Philadelphia Eagles and the Green Bay Packers. He was a first ballot electee to the NFL Hall of Fame on February 4, 2006 and enshrined on August 5 of that year, sadly, two years after his untimely death at the age of 43 in 2004.

He had 1,112 career tackles in the NFL, along with 198 sacks and 3 interceptions. Name a player who has been that impactful and dominant. Go ahead, make my day. Name one!

Photo courtesy of the Philadelphia Eagles

#92 · REGGIE WHITE
Tennessee • Hgt: 6-5 • Wgt: 300 • Born: December 19, 1961
Died: December 26, 2004

Position: Defensive End
15-Year NFL Career
Eagles 8 Years (1985-1992)

"He was the best defensive end I've ever seen," said Ray Didinger. "Gino Marchetti was before my time, but I saw lots of Deacon Jones, who was a great player. Reggie was big and strong and quicker than any defensive end I saw. He combined strength and quickness, which resulted in flat-out dominance."

While playing for the Volunteers in Tennessee, White had accumulated 293 tackles, 201 of which were solo, 32 sacks, 19 tackles-for-loss and 7 batted-down passes. White's "Minister of Defense" moniker is more than just a clever name for a great defensive player. During his years at Tennessee, White became involved with the Fellowship of Christian Athletes and was actually ordained a Baptist Minister.

When he graduated in 1983, the upstart Memphis Showboats of the United States Football League (USFL) came calling. His first experience with professional football was every bit as overpowering as any other of his football experiences. White's two seasons in Memphis saw him start 36 games, with 198 tackles, 23.5 sacks and 7 forced fumbles.

With the end of the USFL in 1985, a door opened for Reggie White—a door to the National Football League. White signed with the Philadelphia Eagles, who owned his rights, and an eight-year love affair began. He was an immediate impact player as his Birds' statistics indicate. He amassed 124 sacks in those eight years, making him the all-time Eagles sack leader. He set the single-season record of 21 sacks in 1987. White became the only player to ever accumulate 20 sacks in 12 games. And amazingly, as a Philadelphia Eagle, he had more sacks than games played.

After the 1992 season, White and the Eagles were unable to agree on a contractual agreement. White became a free agent and signed with the Green Bay Packers. During his six-year tenure on the Frozen Tundra, he accumulated 68.5 additional sacks. He was also a key factor in the team's success that led to a pair of Super Bowl appearances, including a victory in Super Bowl XXXI. It was the one championship of Reggie White's career.

He retired following the 1998 season, after being honored as the NFL Defensive Player of the Year. Following a year away from the game, he returned for one last go 'round with the Carolina Panthers in 2000. White played in 16 games, recording 5.5 sacks. He quit for good following that season.

White found himself in the middle of controversy in 1998 after appearing on the ABC television show, 20/20. During an interview he made critical comments about gays and lesbians, based on his religious beliefs. He appeared in a newspaper advertising campaign that tried to convince gays and lesbians that they could cease their homosexuality. CBS eventually withdrew its five-year, $6 million contract for White to be part of its pre-game show after he called homosexuality a sin.

"I liked Reggie a lot," said Didinger. "His faith, his Christianity meant a lot to him. He wore his faith on his sleeve. The thing was, whether you agree or disagree, Reggie was genuine about his faith. We talked about it a lot. Not only did he talk the talk, but he walked the walk. He followed through. That defined his life. He regarded his work with the Church and his faith as the most important part of his life. He believed that God gave him the ability to be the football player he was because he could then create a platform to deliver his message."

Didinger recalled an instance where he wanted to write a feature story about White and his former teammate, Herb Lusk, a minister in Philadelphia. Quite often on Fridays when the Eagles had a shortened practice, White and Lusk would distribute food to the poor and preach the Gospel. White agreed to let Didinger come along, but only if he did not write about the tradition. He didn't want or need the publicity.

"One thing that people don't realize about Reggie is that he was really funny," Didinger said. "He was seen as a solemn person and he was solemn, but boy was he funny. He did some of the best imitations and impersonations. Reggie did Muhammad Ali perfectly. He also loved wrestling and could imitate all of the wrestlers. And he did a great Rodney Dangerfield."

On a football Sunday, December 26, 2004, Reggie White was rushed from his home to a hospital in Huntersville, North Carolina, where he was pronounced dead. He had suffered a fatal cardiac arrhythmia. The Medical Examiner found that the most likely cause of death was cardiac and pulmonary sarcoidosis. Sleep apnea may have also contributed to his death at the age of 43.

Regardless of any controversy caused by his beliefs, there is absolutely no controversy about Reggie White's impact and talent on the football field. His widow, Sara White, delivered her husband's acceptance speech at his NFL Hall of Fame induction ceremony in 2006.

White was also named to the Wisconsin Athletic Hall of Fame in 2005 and the Philadelphia Sports Hall of Fame in 2007.

Chapter Eight

THE DEFENSIVE LINE

DENNIS HARRISON

D ennis "Big Foot" Harrison made quite an impact as a pass rushing defensive end for the Eagles. Drafted in the fourth round out of Vanderbilt, he played sparingly as a rookie. But every appearance added to his experience and prepared him for his future as a dominating presence on the defensive line.

In his sophomore season in 1979, injuries slowed his progress. But he moved into the starting lineup in 1980 and became an impact player on the defensive line. Playing at left defensive end, he accumulated 56 solo tackles, nine sacks, six deflected passes, and 28 quarterback hurries. Dennis "Big Foot" Harrison let it be known that he was a force to be reckoned with for opposing offensive linemen.

When Dennis Harrison was on the field, quite often, opposing quarterbacks knew they had to get rid of the ball quickly.

In the NFC Championship victory, his recovery of Dallas QB Danny White's fumble at the Cowboy 11 led to a field goal that broke a 7-7 tie in the third quarter. And of course, that was the year the Eagles played in the Super Bowl.

"I thought that year was the best, as far as my career," said Harrison. "As a team, we felt that nobody was going to stop us. Playing in the Super Bowl was great. It didn't take long to get over it. But we did feel that we were the better team. But turnovers and big plays hurt us.

Denis O'Keefe/Philadelphia Daily News

#68 · DENNIS HARRISON
Vanderbilt • Hgt: 6-8 • Wgt: 275 • Born: July 31, 1956

**Position: Defensive End
10-Year NFL Career
Eagles Seven Years (1978-1984)**

"We were just out of sync. It was doing the same thing in practice for two weeks. It just threw us off our system."

The 1981 season was a good one for Harrison, but it was a year in which the team suffered a tremendous heartbreak with a wild-card loss to the New York Giants in the playoffs.

The following year, Big Foot fought back a challenge from first-round draft pick Leonard Mitchell. All he did was answer the challenge with 10.5 sacks and 66 tackles in a nine-game season that was cut short by a players' strike. That year, Dennis Harrison received his greatest individual award, being a UPI second-team All-NFC selection and was chosen for the Pro Bowl for the only time in his ten-year NFL career.

He was a popular figure on the Eagles squad.

"You go around town and people point you out," he said. "I thought the city and the fans were great. I never met a bad fan there. Those fans are just the best. Philadelphia is a great sports town."

Harrison also played for the Los Angeles Rams, the San Francisco 49ers and the Atlanta Falcons. Since his playing days ended, he has remained in football, passing along his knowledge as a coach. He spent five years at his alma mater, Vanderbilt. He now teaches health and physical education and coaches at Brentwood Middle School in Nashville.

Where Have You Gone?

DON HULTZ

Throughout most of his twelve years in the National Football League, Don Hultz was a quiet and unassuming defensive end who let his actions on the playing field do his talking. He was a powerful performer who made his presence felt on the field and who still holds a National Football League record.

During his rookie campaign with the Minnesota Vikings, this free agent from Southern Mississippi set the record for most opponents' fumbles recovered in a season with nine. The only other player with nine fumble recoveries in a season is former Seattle Seahawks quarterback Dave Krieg. But that was quite different, as Krieg recovered nine of his own fumbles in 1989.

So while Hultz had a long and successful career, it is his first season in which he gained the most notoriety.

"I was a free agent who was at the right place at the right time in Minnesota," Hultz said. "I'm proud of the record, but at the time it was no big issue. I was fortunate enough to create a few turnovers for my teammates and was able to recover a few myself. I didn't have much of a history for that. I played on defense and offense at Southern Mississippi and caught a couple of touchdown passes. But not many fumbles."

Ironically, Hultz's ninth fumble recovery came against the Philadelphia Eagles in the Vikings' season finale, when he fell on a fumble

#83 · DON HULTZ

Southern Mississippi • Hgt: 6-3 • Wgt: 245 • Born: December 16, 1940

Position: Defensive End
12-Year NFL Career
Eagles 10 Years (1964-1973)

by quarterback Sonny Jurgensen. It was ironic because Hultz, known as "The Magnet" was traded to the Eagles that off season along with Ray Poage, Chuck Lawson and Terry Kosens in exchange for talented running back Ted Dean.

Hultz had a long tenure with the Eagles, but he was with the team during some lean years. He didn't expect a trade after a successful rookie season but found the Philadelphia area enjoyable.

"Philadelphia is a great city," he said. "But I was kind of surprised by the trade and a little disappointed to be part of a four-for-one trade. We went to the Runner-Up Bowl and made some trades, bringing in Mike Ditka and Gary Ballman. We were supposed to go to the championship. But there were some contract problems, some coaching changes and things deteriorated.

"Right before he was let go, the fans were throwing snowballs at Coach Joe Kuharich. There was a little hostility. But like all fans, they expected a winner. If you lose, it's disappointing. They're typical fans in Philadelphia.

"But I had no problem with the city. Like a lot of players, we lived in New Jersey."

After his initial nine fumble recoveries in 1963, Hultz had just three more in the next 11 seasons. He proved to be a versatile player who was also able to play at linebacker.

"I liked pass defense, "Hultz said. "I played one year at linebacker. I wasn't the biggest guy. I had to depend on my speed and mobility. It's always disappointing to lose. But so many factors go into it. You just do the best you can and hope for the best and that tomorrow brings better things."

Don Hultz is in the record books in the NFL and was also voted to the University of Southern Mississippi's Team of the Century. Though quiet, his play spoke loudly. He had a fulfilling career in football.

"The personal accomplishment was the biggest thing," he said. "I went up there as a free agent and was at the right place at the right time and made the Vikings team. Then I continued my career longer than most and never had a major injury. My philosophy was that I'd do my best and give 100 percent all the time. "

After his playing days ended, Hultz went into law enforcement, working for the attorney general's office as a criminal investigator near Memphis for 21 years. He is now retired and keeps himself occupied by farming.

TIM ROSSOVICH

E very now and then a player impacts a city and a sports franchise in a way that transcends time. As a first-round draft pick taken out of the University of Southern California by the Eagles in 1968, much was expected from All-America defensive end Tim Rossovich. Nearly 50 years later, it's fair to say that Rosso didn't disappoint, as his outstanding play on the field and wild antics off the field are the still the stuff of legends.

Known for his ferocious play and crazy stunts, it's important to remember that first and foremost, Tim Rossovich was a talented, loyal and dedicated football player and teammate.

"If you ask any of my teammates, they'll tell you that I was the first one on the field and the last one to leave," Rossovich said from his home in California. "I gave 150 or 200 percent on the field. I tried to do well and be a support for everyone I respected and worked for, my teammates. Football is the closest thing to combat that you'll ever find. You depend on each other, and everybody has to do their job. You support one another. The game is a web you weave together with your heart, soul and mind. Otherwise, it doesn't work."

A native of the west coast, Rossovich was unsure of what to expect from the Eagles, the area or the fans. But he quickly became a favorite in his new home.

Photo courtesy of the Philadelphia Eagles

#82 · TIM ROSSOVICH
USC • Hgt: 6-5 • Wgt: 230 • Born: March 14, 1946

Position: Defensive End / Linebacker
Seven-Year NFL Career
Eagles Four Years (1968-1971)

"I honestly knew nothing of the east coast," he said. "I didn't know what to expect, but I was happy and proud to have been drafted in the first round. It was just great to be considered that high, that's your dream. I had the God-given gifts and the ability to set the foundation for the rest of my life. It was time to see how far I could go.

"Philly is probably the best and the worst town to play football in. The fans are behind you 1,000 percent until you make a mistake. They are probably the most aggressive fans in the country. But I have wonderful memories of them. They were very endearing to me and very supportive of me.

"I went to a concert at the Spectrum for the Rolling Stones. They called me up on stage and I got more attention than Mick Jagger. It's a blue-collar, honest town. The best experiences I had were with the people."

There were few players more popular in Philadelphia than Rossovich and his buddy, defensive back Bill Bradley. But there was considerable social change underway in society, and professional football was probably one of the entities that was least willing to change with the times. Former tackle Ed Khayat of Tulane was the Eagles head coach. While he wanted his players to wear short hair, be cleanshaven and obey a dress code, Rosso went in another direction.

"They just didn't understand the changes from the decades before," Rossovich said. "It was the '60s and people had long hair and facial hair. I didn't understand why hair and dress codes were so important. They had nothing to do with your performance on the field. I was very professional toward my job and very committed to my teammates."

You would be hard pressed to find a former teammate without praise for the dedication Tim Rossovich brought to the game, his ability and appreciation for his fun behavior.

"He was an absolute nut," said fellow defensive end Mel Tom. "Tim and I played on opposite sides of the defensive line. I'll tell you, he was smart and could move. He just lacked size."

"When I first met Tim, he bit on a glass and starting chewing it up," said running back Cyril Pinder. "I'd never seen anything like that. He was part of that wild bunch from Southern Cal. Tim was a great athlete and I respect him immensely. He was one of the toughest players I remember. I enjoyed playing with him. He kept us all loose."

"In my opinion, Tim was the most colorful character I ever had the privilege of playing with," said former teammate, kicker Happy Feller. "He was one of a kind, really different. But he was a helluva ballplayer. A great talent and a real good guy."

"He was the most talented big man I ever knew," said quarterback Norm Snead. "He was also the craziest man I ever knew. Absolutely fearless. He was strong and talented, fun and exciting."

On the subject of being committed, Tim Rossovich kept his teammates loose with his antics off the playing field. In addition to eating glass, he set himself on fire, jumped off of a ladder into a whirlpool and hid in an ice machine. Once he kept a bird in his mouth during a team meeting and when the coach asked for questions, Rosso opened his mouth, releasing the bird.

While management had some problems with his behavior, his teammates and fans were supportive. And it really did loosen up the squad.

"It was a different time," he said. "I wanted people to acknowledge me. Boy, did I get attention. Losing was distressing, and we worked very hard to try to win. It was about everybody getting off their asses and doing something to try to win some football games."

The Birds of that era didn't win that many gridiron contests, but Rossovich improved as a player and eventually moved to linebacker, where he excelled and his size was more conducive to success. He still enjoyed the experience, win or lose.

"You can win four or five games a year and still have wonderful memories," he said.

Rossovich was different and at times defiant. But no matter what, he was interesting.

"He was certainly different," said Ray Didinger. "I often wondered about how much of his image was real and how much was play acting. Initially, I thought it was just a character he was playing with the capes he'd wear, the long hair and that crazy Rasputin store. The more I was around him the more I thought there was a certain part of him that was wired differently than most people.

"Rossovich was a good player. It's a shame he isn't remembered more for that. There was more to him than just his antics. Early in Tim's career, big Bob Brown was playing tackle for the Rams and Tim went one-on-one with him the whole game. Bob probably weighed 300 pounds and Tim was around 230. But Tim won the battle all day. And that was against Brown, a guy who they said would kill an ant with an axe."

But the problems with the front office eventually saw him moved to the Chargers in San Diego for two years, then the Philadelphia Bell of the World Football League and finally his final stop with the Houston Oilers in 1976.

Following his playing days, Rossovich became a stunt man and actor. Some of his movie credits include *Avenging Angel, The Sting ll, The Long Riders* and *The Main Event.* His television experience includes guest appearances on *Mike Hammer, Baywatch, Hunter, Magnum, P.I., Dallas, MacGyver* and *Charlie's Angels.*

These days, Tim Rossovich is semi-retired and living in Grass Valley, California.

"My life as a football player allowed me to become more of a person than I would have been without it," he said. "I tried to be a great player and a great teammate and someone who the fans remember and cared for. I'd like to be remembered as somebody who respected where he was, what he was doing and the people who he was doing it for. When I look at my time with the Eagles, I think of nothing but joy and pleasure about being there. I am thankful for the opportunity."

MEL TOM

Although big Mel Tom certainly looked like a defensive end at six foot four, 250 lbs., during the early stages of his NFL career with the Eagles he wore at linebacker-like No. 58. Ironically, he was drafted out of San Jose State as a backer, but switched to the front line one day after practice.

"We had our training camp in Hershey, and I had a pretty good feeling about making the team," Tom said from his native Hawaii, where he returned following his career. "I had never really played defensive end very much. I got drafted as a linebacker. That's why I had No. 58. But because of my height, I guess they thought I was too tall to be a linebacker. So one day after practice they had me try defensive end, which was a position they were a little short on. The liked what they saw and moved me."

While he switched to a more imposing No. 99 a few years later, Mel Tom made his presence felt from the defensive end position on the field. Not familiar with the city or the team, he quickly became accustomed to both.

"I knew nothing at all about Philadelphia," he said. "It was a completely foreign country to me. Some people from San Jose told me it was a tough team. I really didn't even know what pro football was like. I had seen a few 49ers games at old Keysar Stadium, but that was about

Photo courtesy of the Philadelphia Eagles

#58 · #99 · MEL TOM
San Jose State • Hgt: 6-4 • Wgt: 250 • Born: August 4, 1941
Died: April 27, 2006

Position: Defensive End
Nine-Year NFL Career
Eagles Seven Years (1967-1973)

it. I was happy coming there. It's your job. I enjoyed the game and the friends I made and really liked the city and the life."

Tom was a real competitor who seemed to save some of his hardest-hitting impact games against some great quarterbacks like Roger Staubach of Dallas and Fran Tarkenton of the New York Giants. In addition to being a strong physical specimen, Tom had the proper mental approach that helped him succeed.

"I had some pretty good games against Dallas and Tarkenton," he said. "The game is 50 percent physical and 50 percent mental. The hardest part is the mental game. You have to get psyched up for the game. The people who can really focus and get psyched are the All-Pros. Take a guy like Dick Butkus. When I played with him in Chicago, he was a really nice guy until you broke the huddle. When it was time to play defense, he psyched himself up."

Mel Tom is still fondly remembered for his play and his personality in the locker room. The Eagles of those days may not have won as often as they would have liked, but they appreciated each other and the honest effort each player made.

"Mel's nickname was The Pineapple because of where he was from," said defensive back Bill Bradley. "He was a stubborn old Hawaiian who was a heckuva defensive lineman and a pretty good player. I remember the time he nailed Roger Staubach after I picked off a pass. Mel was a good football player."

Tom never enjoyed a winning season with the Eagles, as he was part of what seemed like an endless rebuilding process. But he enjoyed his time with the team and took a liking to the area. Following his career in Philadelphia, he finished up with the Bears in Chicago.

"I think that Mel Tom had the ability to be the best defensive end that ever played in Philadelphia," said former GM Pete Retzlaff. "The potential was there. He was certainly good, but he could have been a lot better. He could have been the best."

When football ended, Mel Tom returned to Hawaii as he had done in every off season, to stay. After spending time as a commercial salmon fisherman, he opened and operated a tavern.

While it became in vogue for today's generation of football people to criticize Veteran's Stadium, Tom was a real fan of the Eagles' former home.

"I just loved the Vet," he said. "My first stadium in the pros was Franklin Field, which was a terrible place. The locker room was awful, but the field was okay. It was just old. The Vet was beautiful, brand new with great facilities. Soldier Field in Chicago was a lot like Franklin Field.

"I was back in Philly a couple of years ago and I was shocked about how it looked. Wonderfully shocked. When I played there were winos all around Market Street and Broad Street. Now it's a really nice cosmopolitan area, almost like a tourist trap. I was really happy with what I saw."

Tom hoped he'd be remembered for his effort and enthusiasm.

"I really enjoyed the life and making new friends," he said. "I'd just like to be thought of as a happy Hawaiian."

Sadly, the happy Hawaiian passed away of heart failure on April 27, 2006.

Chapter Nine

THE LINEBACKERS

Where Have You Gone?

MAXIE BAUGHAN

When the Eagles drafted this All-America linebacker and center from Georgia Tech in the second round of the 1960 draft, they knew they had a player. But just how good Maxie Baughan became, earning the first of nine Pro Bowl selections in his rookie year, had to be a pleasant surprise.

In his fourth game in the Eagles' championship season against the Detroit Lions, he had 15 tackles (10 unassisted) and broke up three passes. Then in the crucial meeting against the Giants at New York, he had another six unassisted tackles. And in the season finale at Washington, he had 17 tackles (12 unassisted) and an interception. Not bad for a rookie.

"I was scared to death," Baughan said of his rookie season with the Eagles. "Norm Van Brocklin was the quarterback. Chuck Bednarik was there. Some of those guys were old enough to be my dad. I had never even seen a professional football game until I played in one.

"I always loved Philadelphia. The people made the city and they were so gracious to the Eagle football players. They accepted us, but of course, we were winning. I made the Pro Bowl that year as a rookie, which was a great way to start."

Photo courtesy of the Philadelphia Eagles

#55 · MAXIE BAUGHAN
Georgia Tech • Hgt: 6-1 • Wgt: 230 • Born: August 3, 1938

Position: Linebacker
11-Year NFL Career
Eagles Six Years (1960-1965)

The Birds captured their only title that year with Baughan, a rookie, at outside linebacker. The team lost its first game of the season, but things gradually started to jell.

"We lost our first game and then the coach, Buck Shaw, gave his famous speech about it being like a bus station there. We sort of just fell into it that year. We didn't have a championship team personnel-wise, but we did team-wise and chemistry-wise. There was so much leadership from Buck Shaw and from the players.

"If I would have known that the '60 team would be my only championship team, I don't know if I could have enjoyed or cherished it any more than I did. I did everything I could to make it special."

But after the Eagles beat Green Bay in the title game, both Shaw and Van Brocklin retired. Being at the top of the standings affects draft selections, and the Birds began a retreat to the middle of the pack. Even though the team was floundering, Maxie Baughan continued to serve notice that he was one of the premier outside linebackers in the game.

He made the Pro Bowl team again in 1961, '63, '64 and '65. But his frustration mounted with the Eagles. Unfortunately, a dispute over salary, as well as a reported difference of opinion with assistant Dick Evans's defensive strategy, caused Maxie to demand a trade following the '65 season. His preference was to join the expansion Atlanta Falcons, which would have returned him to the city where he had experienced his college success. Rather, he was dealt to the Los Angeles Rams for LB Fred Brown and DT Frank Molden, both of whom quickly faded from the Philadelphia landscape.

While Baughan felt he needed a change, he has nothing but kind words for the fans of Philadelphia.

"My six years that I played there, I could not want to be treated any better than I was," he said. "The fans were always great to me, and I always thought that Philadelphia was very special. I won't knock the L.A. fans, but they were different. It was personal with Philadelphia fans. The Rams fans were supportive, but not as personal.

"The trade was what I needed. We weren't going anywhere and we were losing players. I felt like it was time for a change of scenery. I was frustrated with everything, first of all, myself.

"As far as my career is concerned, the trade to the Rams was one of the best decisions I ever made, playing for George Allen. He trained me for a career in coaching. It was a Godsend."

After leaving the Birds, Maxie Baughan continued to thrive on the West Coast, earning All-Pro honors from 1966 to 1969. While his teams made the playoffs, he would retire with only the 1960 championship season. He retired to become a coach after the 1970 season, including a stint as a player/coach with Allen and the Redskins in 1974.

In his successful second career as a coach, Baughan has shared his expertise in Washington, Baltimore two times, Detroit, Minnesota, Tampa, and he also served as head coach at Cornell.

Retired since 1998, he spends time playing golf, enjoying his grandchildren and spending time with his church groups and teaching youngsters at some football camps near his Maryland home.

He hopes to be remembered as a leader on the football field. All these years later, Maxie Baughan has nothing but appreciation for all that the game of football has done for him.

"I had the opportunity to be a football coach," he said. "It was my livelihood. I got a degree and didn't have to work a day for the rest of my life. I was doing something I loved, playing and coaching football. I was fortunate enough to be able to do that and feel like I never worked a day in my life. And I give George Allen the credit."

There are many people who feel that to give Maxie Baughan the credit he deserves as a football player and coach, that he should be enshrined at the Football Hall of Fame in Canton, Ohio.

Where Have You Gone?

BILL BERGEY

F ormer Eagles owner Leonard Tose believed that a real impact player at the middle linebacker position would bring a Super Bowl victory to Philadelphia. While the popular owner was able to allow his football people to assemble a team that at least reached the big game, it took a little more than just one player to achieve that level of success.

That being said, it's also fair to say that had the Eagles never acquired Bill Bergey to play middle linebacker, they would not have gotten to the Super Bowl. The heart and soul of the Birds defense in the years leading up to the 1980 season was an All-American at Arkansas State, where he set five school defensive records that still stand today. In 1976, fans voted Bergey the top player in Arkansas State history.

Before coming to Philadelphia, Bergey spent the first five years of his career in Cincinnati with the Bengals playing for Paul Brown.

"He was a great coach," Bergey said. "He was quiet and soft spoken. He was the type of person who didn't mind physical mistakes, but he hated mental mistakes. He was quite an innovator who invented the face mask. But he didn't want any stupid players on his team, so he instituted testing for a while to measure the intelligence of his football players. They were some really goofy tests that were eventually stopped thanks to the Players Association."

Photo courtesy of the Philadelphia Eagles

#66 · BILL BERGEY
Arkansas State • Hgt: 6-2 • Wgt: 250 • Born: February 9, 1945

Position: Linebacker
12-Year NFL Career
Eagles Seven Years (1974-1980)

But Bergey's relationship with Brown and the Bengals cooled when the upstart World Football League came knocking with bushels of money to spend on top NFL players, including Larry Czonka, Jim Kiick, Paul Warfield and Bill Bergey. A long and acrimonious situation ensued between the Bengals and Bergey, who was eventually dealt to the Eagles in exchange for first-round draft picks in 1977 and '78 as well as a second-round pick in '78.

"On July 14, 1974, the day the WFL had its first game in Philadelphia at old JFK Stadium, I signed with the Eagles," Bergey said. "At first I wasn't sure that I wanted to go to Philadelphia. I knew it was the home of the Liberty Bell and they had something called soft pretzels and losing football. Plus, Mike McCormick, the coach, had testified against me in court as a favor to Paul Brown. But Leonard Tose was very, very persistent about me coming to the Philadelphia Eagles. He honestly thought that all he needed to win the Super Bowl was a middle linebacker.

"My impressions of the city were great. I developed a real nice love affair with the people of Philadelphia. I never tried to come off like a big timer or anything. And believe me, you will meet the same people on the way down that you do on the way up. So I always tried to treat people the way that I'd like to be treated."

Eagles fans were notorious for their reputation of not treating most visiting and even some home players nicely. For Bergey's money, that bad reputation is very much overstated.

"All the fans want is a winner and to see effort from the players," he said. "They are no different from any other fans. We're just a little bit louder. There are just wonderful people in this area. I could have settled anywhere after my career ended. But I love Philadelphia. To this day, staying in Philadelphia was the best thing I've ever done."

In addition to trading for Bergey, one of the best things that Leonard Tose ever did was bring in Dick Vermeil as coach. Make no mistake, he worked his players hard.

"When he started out, he was just killing us," Bergey said. "His philosophy was to tear an athlete down and then build him up after the season starts. He got rid of a lot of dead meat on our team. Only a handful of us were left.

"He is a super buddy of mine. I was the first player who ever invited him to their home for dinner. He brought a bottle of wine and got all choked up. It meant a lot to him."

The Eagles reached the Super Bowl following the 1980 season and just had an incredibly frustrating game in New Orleans where they simply couldn't get started. While there was some debate if the team was tired because Vermeil practiced them too hard, Bergey feels that the team's schedule had nothing to do with the flat Super Bowl appearance.

"It wasn't a case of being tired," he said. "We put so much emphasis on the NFC Championship Game against Dallas, it was almost like the Super Bowl was an afterthought. We just couldn't get back up to the same level that we had. We did not get the same emotional level that we did against Dallas. You can try to blame it on pink panties or apple sauce, or anything you want. We just didn't play well and couldn't get clicking."

Troubled by a knee injury, Bergey retired after the Super Bowl defeat to a very successful life after football. He has worked in television and radio as well as Lubert and Adler Investments in Philadelphia and GF Management.

Acquaintances told him to beware of the real world after football. But life after football has been a dream for Bill Bergey. "The real world was pro football," he said. "After retiring, I live in a fantasy world. My life is wonderful."

While he doesn't let the Super Bowl loss eat away at him, it's hard not to think about losing the big game. It was to be his only shot at football immortality.

"I really wanted to win one more game," Bergey said. "It wasn't about rings or anything like that. But just to say that you won a championship would have been the greatest thing in the world. Just to win one. Now I'd just like to be remembered as a linebacker who lined up on every single play and gave it everything I had.

"Life is so wonderful, but it goes by so darn fast, it makes me crazy. But life in Philadelphia is wonderful."

Where Have You Gone?

JOHN BUNTING

I f there is one word to describe what former Eagles linebacker John Bunting is all about, that word would have to be "respect." He respected the game, those who played it, the coaches and also the fans. His attitude and dedication to the game helped this 10th round draft choice start 119 of his 133 career NFL games.

"I was just a hard-working guy who gave everything he had each and every day," Bunting said from his office at North Carolina, where he serves as the Tar Heels head coach. "I loved our football program and our team. And I loved the city of Philadelphia. I could really relate to the hard-working, blue-collar ethic of that city and that team."

After a successful career as a player at North Carolina, where Bunting's final team won the ACC Championship, he had a new experience with his introduction to Philadelphia, where the team was not nearly as successful.

"Philly was a shock," he said. "I went from playing for the ACC Champions to losing and getting booed. But it was a great experience to be part of the Philadelphia sports scene. They love their sports up there. They embrace a team that puts out. They look for effort from their players. The blue-collar teams are their favorite.

"I'm still very close with Billy Cunningham, the former Sixers coach who is a good friend. There were a lot of prominent sports figures in

Photo courtesy of the Philadelphia Eagles

#95 · JOHN BUNTING
North Carolina • Hgt: 6-1 • Wgt: 220 • Born: July 15, 1950

Position: Linebacker
11-Year NFL Career
Eagles 11 Years (1972-1982)
Two Years USFL Philadelphia Stars

that town, such as Mike Schmidt, Bill Barber, Bobby Clarke and Rick MacLeish. It was quite a decade of playing sports in Philadelphia. And we went from a very poor team to a good team under Dick Vermeil. The whole city got behind their teams."

As the Eagles started to become a more successful team, Bunting had a serious knee injury during the 1978 season. Many players didn't recover from the type of major surgery he endured, having cartilage removed and ligaments repaired in his knee. But return he did, as Bunting and his tenacious defensive partners jelled as a unit and helped the Eagles get to football's promised land, the Super Bowl, in 1980.

"John was like a coach on the field," said former teammate Guy Morriss. "He was an extremely studious player who was our signal caller on defense. He kept everybody loose and was quite a cut up and clown. But he was very serious when it came to football."

On the road to the Super Bowl, the Birds beat the dastardly Dallas Cowboys in the NFC Championship game at a frigid Veterans Stadium. That victory was one of John Bunting's career highlights.

"I'll never forget beating Dallas in the NFC Championship game in sub-zero weather," he said. "Winning the championship was something that our fans wanted for so long. It was a magical year, but we didn't build the year with magic. Dick Vermeil's idea was that you go on the field and you get better every day.

"Then we had the opportunity to play in The Game. It was something that probably didn't sink in until a week or two after the Super Bowl. I don't think any of us were ashamed, but we were disappointed. To this day, many of us regret the way we played but rejoice in getting there."

Bunting stuck with the Eagles through the 1982 season and then spent the next two years with the Philadelphia Stars of the USFL. His knowledge, love and respect for the game got him into coaching. He has been an assistant coach with the Baltimore Stars, Brown University, Kansas City Chiefs and New Orleans Saints. He was also head coach at Glassboro State University from 1988 through 1992, sporting a 38-12-1 record and with North Carolina from 2001-2006, with a 27-45 mark.

"I was actually in the Philadelphia area for 20 years," he said. "Thirteen were spent as a player and then coaching at Glassboro State, which is now Rowan University. It's my second home. I miss Philly and I hope to visit often. That's a place where I grew all the way up, learning what it takes to win under Dick Vermeil. In the environment up there, losing is not tolerated.

"Football takes a special breed of athlete and a special breed of team to win. The Patriots are that type of team. I've had some really good coaches, and I realize just how tough coaching is and how competitive it is. Vermeil set a very high standard. What he enjoyed is what I enjoy, the relationship you develop with the players and your fellow coaches, as well as the fan base."

Some of the lessons he learned deal with honesty and integrity.

"You have to have a tremendous amount of discipline," Bunting said. "You must also learn the difference between telling the truth and being fair. It's very important for players to know you are telling them the truth, but the truth might not be fair. You have to be consistent. That's the type of player I was, and you need that to be a coach."

John Bunting now works as a commentator and announcer for college football.

MIKE REICHENBACH

L ike so many Philadelphia sports teams that earn the respect of the city's tough fans, free agent linebacker Mike Reichenbach was an overachiever who left everything he had on the playing field. After his rookie season under Marion Campbell and Fred Bruney, he became one of Buddy's Boys, playing for the defensive guru of the Chicago Bears, Buddy Ryan.

"Buddy called me into the office to meet with me," Reichenbach said. "In his scheme, we made all of our adjustments at the line, and I had to study to make sure I knew what he wanted me to do. After I passed all of his tests, he told me I had to come into camp in the best shape of my life. He worked us really hard. He broke us down and then built us back up again. I learned a lot from him. Some of the things he implemented I still use today. He had a lot of great concepts and he was tough.

"He demanded a lot. The middle linebacker had a lot of responsibilities. He really loved his big guys, the defensive linemen. Buddy put together a good group of guys. It was an exciting time to play for the Eagles. We had an attack defense instead of a defense that bent but didn't break."

Much like the Stanley Cup champion Philadelphia Flyers of the '70s, the Eagles played hard, tough football and arrived at the point of

AP/WWP

#55 · MIKE REICHENBACH
East Straudsberg • Hgt: 6-2 • Wgt: 240 • Born: September 14, 1961

Position: Linebacker
Nine-Year NFL Career
Eagles Six Years (1984-1989)

impact in ill humor. Reichenbach fit right in on the field and off. As a kid who grew up rooting for the rough and tumble Pittsburgh Steelers, he enjoyed his time with the Eagles and liked the city and its fans.

"It was a great place to play," he said. "There was passion there unlike in Miami, where football was kind of an afterthought. The fans got a bad rap sometimes. They are there every week and when they're behind you, it's like a 12th man. It's a tough place to play as an opposing player. The fans are really hard on opposing teams. They support you but demand a whole lot. It was really a fun time."

Reichenbach was a member of those teams that dominated during the regular season, but had difficulties in the playoffs. The Fog Bowl in Soldier Field in Chicago was one of the games that got away.

"I was one of the captains of the team and the officials said that as long as we could see the goal posts we could play. But who could see the goal posts? That game was an advantage for the Bears. They were a strong running team and we weren't very innovative on offense. We kind of depended on Randall Cunningham to make something happen. But their ends boxed Randall in. It was a hard game."

Following six successful seasons in Philadelphia, Reichenbach then played for two years in Miami with the Dolphins before finishing up with the 49ers in 1992.

"Each organization has its own personality," he said. "There were some things about the Eagles where you didn't always get treated well and the facilities were not the greatest. Miami was a different mentality. Don Shula surrounded himself with really good people. He was a hands-on coach who also allowed his coaches to coach.

"The best organization was the 49ers. Everything they did they did like they expected to be in the Super Bowl. With the Eagles, we were slugging to get out of the NFC East."

While he was not a star, or the type of player who was expected to be an All-Pro, his overachieving nature made him a favorite with the fans. Since success didn't come easily, you get the feeling that he got more out of his career than a golden boy, high draft pick.

"I guess if you look at my bio, I shouldn't have made it," he said. "That made me appreciate things more. I got to replace Bill Cowler when he got hurt and won a spot on special teams. In my first game against the Redskins, I made all the tackles on special teams.

"I prepared for every game, never missed a game and was ready to play. I look at football as the thing that enabled me to walk away and give my life to Christ. I look at it as a positive experience because that brought me to God. It developed my faith and enabled me to walk away on my own terms."

Now Mike Reichenbach works for National Label, a company that provides labels for pharmaceutical companies. He also is involved in various ministries and coaches football at Calvary Christian Academy in Philadelphia.

"I love to work with kids," he said. "Football was a job that ran its course. I found something better now, serving God. It's allowed me to not look back, but to press on. I'm a devoted husband and father. As a player, I gave everything I had and I laid it out on the field. I didn't have the great athletic ability, but I did my best."

STEVE ZABEL

S teve Zabel came to the Eagles in the first round of the 1970 draft, the sixth player chosen. Coming from an outstanding college program at Oklahoma, he had big game experience with the Sooners who won two Big 8 Championships and appeared in the Orange Bowl during his three varsity years.

In Philadelphia, Zabel became part of a rebuilding program under Coach Jerry Williams, that would include a 3-10-1 rookie season.

"I was elated to be picked so early," Zabel said. "I really hoped to go to Denver or Minnesota, which was closer to where I was from, and I could play in the cold weather. I had no idea that Philadelphia was going to draft me. But I'm glad it happened the way it did.

"I loved Philadelphia. It's one of the greatest sports towns ever. It's a blue-collar town and the fans were great to me. They're very knowledgeable and they knew who the football players were and who weren't football players. If you don't have pride, there is nothing to play for. It was a long, hard year that was very frustrating for me. I got kicked out of three games for fighting. The reality was that we didn't have a very good team.

"But I started half of the games and they were the games we won. We even beat Miami."

AP Photo/Bill Ingraham

#89 · STEVE ZABEL
Oklahoma • Hgt: 6-4 • Wgt: 240 • Born: March 20, 1948

Position: Linebacker / Tight End
10-Year NFL Career
Eagles Five Years (1970-1974)

When Zabel played at Oklahoma for Coach Chuck Fairbanks, he played both ways as a junior. In addition to tight end, he was also a linebacker for the Sooners. The Eagles coaching staff realized that Zabel might be better served playing on defense, rather than on a lousy offensive football team.

So he made the switch to outside linebacker and people began to take notice. The Birds got off to an 0-3 start in 1971 and Williams was let go and replaced by Ed Khayat. The team responded with a 6-3-1 record in the final ten games of the season to give hope for the future.

"I came to camp that year full of confidence and in excellent physical conditioning and shape," Zabel said. "Ed Khayat replaced Coach Williams and everyone took to Eddie that first year. He was a player's coach, a man's man. He was also hilarious. We showed great promise for the next year. I really played well, and defensively we did well in 1971. Bill Bradley made the All-Pro team and I thought I played well enough to make the All-Pro team as well."

The hope for the future soon faded to black as the '72 team went 2-11-1 amid much dissension in the ranks, which included holdouts, unpopular trades and an edict from Khayat, who changed from the previous season.

Tim Rossovich and Bradley held out for more money. The team signed Bradley, but dealt Rossovich to San Diego. Then they moved Zabel from outside linebacker to middle linebacker, a position he felt uncomfortable with.

"After they traded Tim to San Diego, one of the coaches, Jimmy Carr came to me and said that I was a great athlete who they wanted to play middle linebacker," Zabel said. "I should have said that I couldn't play middle linebacker, but in those days you were taught to take the challenge."

Zabel suffered a knee injury after the third exhibition game in an early morning practice, which also saw Lee Bouggess and Gary Pettigrew injured. The following season, he suffered a ruptured Achilles tendon.

Following the 1974 season, Zabel was dealt to New England where he was reunited with his old college coach, Chuck Fairbanks. His four seasons in New England saw the Patriots become a regular playoff team and Steve Zabel helped anchor the defense.

"I'm proud of my career," he said. "Given the circumstances I did the best that I could. I never made All-Pro, but I played as hard as I could on every down. I played for my teammates and tried to win and do my responsibility."

Since his football career ended, Zabel and his wife Susan raised their children and he got involved in the business world. But then he became chairman of the board of a non-profit organization, City Care Inc., which feeds homeless people in Oklahoma. They even instituted a Whiz Kids tutoring program for children.

"It's very, very rewarding," he said. "I decided to try to do something useful rather than trading my time for somebody else's money."

Steve Zabel more than justified being a first-round selection in the National Football League draft. But it's obvious that he is also a first-round selection in life after the game.

Chapter Ten

THE SECONDARY

BILL BRADLEY

S uper Bill Bradley was one of the most popular players ever to wear the Eagles' green, silver and white. Drafted in the third round of the 1969 draft, he was a jack of all trades with the Birds, serving as a safety, special teams player, punter, kick return specialist, holder and emergency quarterback. He was also a master at those trades, earning All-Pro honors at safety in 1971, '72, and '73. He was unquestioningly one of the leaders of a very tough, hard-nosed defensive unit.

Not only that, but Bill Bradley was also the first player in the history of the NFL to lead the league in interceptions in two consecutive seasons, a feat he accomplished by picking off 11 passes in 1971 and nine errant throws in 1972. That feat has been matched only once since Bradley had those two outstanding seasons. The former Texas Longhorne quarterback began his tenure in Philadelphia as a versatile back up, but soon became the starting free safety.

"I was drafted as what they called a punter/player," Bradley said from Baylor University where he was hired as the Bears defensive coordinator in 2004. "I started out as the punter and I backed up both safeties, Nate Ramsey and Joe Scarpati. In Texas, the state motto was The Friendly State, and in Philadelphia it was You've Got a Friend in Pennsylvania.

"I found the people to be very friendly and helpful, like in Texas. Philadelphia was an extremely livable city where people actually lived

Photo courtesy of the Philadelphia Eagles

#28 · BILL BRADLEY
University of Texas • Hgt: 6-0 • Wgt: 180 • Born: January 24, 1947

Position: Defensive Back / Punter
Nine-Year NFL Career
Eagles Eight Years (1969-1976)

in the downtown area. In Texas, people commuted into the city, and it was like a ghost town at night. I lived out on the Main Line in the Devon-Stratford area. There was a wonderful family out there that sort of adopted me, the Calvarese family. They really took me under their wing."

Bradley became a fan favorite on a team that lost more than it won. While often frustrated with the results, he was proud of the effort the team put forth and especially of how the faithful took a liking to his aggressive style of play.

"The fans are fantastic in Philadelphia," he said. "They lived and breathed and died the Eagles. We were bad in those days, but we gave it all we had. On defense, we were a blue-collar unit that really got after people. The fans could be brutal, and we heard our share of boos. But I have the distinction of never being booed there. They never booed me, and I gave them everything I had.

"Losing was very frustrating, especially coming from a highly successful college program. There was a lot of instability around the team, changing players and coaches. We even had an ownership change. After I left, they got real solid with Dick Vermeil. When I was there we always seemed like we were in transition."

Transition or not, Bradley made his presence felt and still holds the Eagles' all-time interception record of 34 picks with Eric Allen. He left the Eagles following the 1976 season and finished up with the Vikings and Cardinals for one season.

"Bill was a great free safety," said former teammate Ben Hawkins. "He had a good eye for the ball and always helped everyone else out there. And people forget, he was a great punt returner."

After retirement, Super Bill stayed in the Philadelphia area in business before returning home to Texas in 1983. A couple of years later he got the coaching bug that is in his family.

"Bill was my roommate my rookie year," said former Eagles kicker Happy Feller. "I had the privilege of playing with him at the University of Texas and with the Eagles. He was a very easygoing guy who never took anything seriously. But he was also your best friend. A very compassionate person who was very sympathetic if you were going through a rough time. That's why he is such a great coach now. He can identify with the players."

Coaching was in Bill Bradley's blood as his father was a very successful baseball coach from the pee-wee to semi-pro level in Texas, with winning seasons in 25 out of 27 years. The Bradley family has

Coaching was in Bill Bradley's blood as his father was a very successful baseball coach from the pee-wee to semi-pro level in Texas, with winning seasons in 25 out of 27 years. The Bradley family has a baseball field named after them as well as the Bradley GT Tank, named after Bill's sixth cousin, Gen. Omar Bradley.

Bradley broke into the coaching ranks with the USFL's San Antonio Gunslingers in 1983 as the team's defensive backs coach and personnel assistant, then spent the 1984 campaign as the club's secondary coach. He then moved on to serve as secondary coach of the USFL's Memphis Showboats (1985) and spent a year coaching at the University of Texas (1987) before moving into the CFL in 1988.

After making coaching stops in Toronto and Calgary, Bradley spent three years as the New York Jets defensive backs coach, followed by several other coaching stints at the college and professional levels.

"Super Bill was a best friend and best teammate," said Tim Rossovich. "He is the nicest and most gentle man in the world. He was one of my best friends, and I think about him many times every day. He's one of the most respected coaches because he understands what the players are going through."

During his tenure at Baylor, Bradley was reunited with his former teammate Guy Morriss, who was the head coach of the Bears. "Guy was my good friend and teammate," Bradley said. "Then I had to call him boss."

In spite of the losing teams, Bill Bradley has nothing but fond memories of his days with the Eagles and hopes the fans feel the same way.

"I would do the same thing again if I had the chance," he said. "I absolutely loved it up there and still enjoy going up there to visit. It is a very friendly city and a great place to be. I'd be glad to be remembered as a hard-working football player who went to work every day with his lunch pail. I was a blue-collar safety who made some interceptions and made and missed some tackles.

"And I never got booed."

Bradley retired from coaching in 2014.

TOM BROOKSHIER

One generation of football fans remember Tom Brookshier as the hard-hitting defensive back who helped the Eagles win the NFL title in 1960. Other generations remember him as the folksy television announcer who teamed with Pat Summerall as possibly the best pairing to ever broadcast football games. But his teammates with the Eagles during his rookie training camp in 1953 had a different impression of Number 40.

"I had never been to Philadelphia," Brookshier said. "My wife and I had just gotten married, we bought a used car and took off in July for training camp. After the first week with just the rookies, the veterans showed up. I needed to make an impression. Our first-round draft pick caught a pass, and I hit him hard and knocked him out. The coach said, 'Great play.' So I knew what I had to do to make the team. The vets got so mad at me because I really hit. They would say that it was just training camp. But it wasn't training camp for me. I was fighting for a job."

Brookshier not only made the team but had eight interceptions during his rookie campaign, making him a fan favorite. Philadelphia's long love affair with Tom Brookshier had begun.

"The city was so big and very friendly," he said. "The fans saw that I was a hitter, and I was accepted right away. Every place I went I was

Photo courtesy of the Philadelphia Eagles

#40 · TOM BROOKSHIER
Colorado • Hgt: 6-0 • Wgt: 196 • Born: December 16, 1931
Died: January 29, 2010

Position: Defensive Back
Seven-Year NFL Career
Eagles Seven Years (1953, 1956-1961)

Brookie the hitter. They accepted me as their guy. Everyone was like family."

After a two-year stint in the air force, Brookshier returned to the team and quickly established himself as one of the best cornerbacks in the game, not just for his pass coverage, but also for his play against the run. He was the defensive signal caller and an inspirational leader on the team.

As the Birds got better, Brookie gained All-Pro recognition in 1959 and '60. The upstart team that won it all reeled off nine straight wins, trailing most of the time at the half. They simply invented ways to win games that were seemingly lost.

"To win nine games in a row was remarkable," he said. "We just found ways to do it. The 2003 Eagles reminded me of the 1960 Eagles. It wasn't just one or two guys that year. Everyone had so much to do with it. Everybody on the team was involved. It was great to be part of that. We all got along and enjoyed the same things. The '61 team was even better. We started off 7-1 and then the injuries hit."

One of the most severe injuries happened to Brookshier, who suffered a compound fracture of his leg against the Chicago Bears. He sat out the following year and was unable to make it back as the injury ended his playing career.

During the final season and a half of Tom Brookshier's playing career, the Birds went 18-3 including the playoffs. "It was like playing in the golden age of football," he said. "Had all of the injuries not hit, we would have gotten to the championship game that second year, too."

Having had experience doing a pregame radio show for two years in 1958 and '59, WCAU hired him as a sports director and commentator on nightly news broadcasts with John Facenda. Then he was paired with Summerall, the first time that two former players were teamed together for football broadcasts.

They had great chemistry between them and took broadcasting the game to new heights by simplifying the game and making it interesting and fun to watch. They were good friends in and out of the broadcasting booth, which made listening to their unique styles even more enjoyable.

"We envisioned a family watching the game on a Sunday afternoon," Brookshier said. "We were like two old football players at a family gathering talking not so much about Xs and Os but how players feel and why the players play better at certain times. It was a different way of looking at football."

After leaving CBS, Brookshier owned a radio station and worked as a consultant for a commercial real estate company.

He was inducted into the Broadcast Pioneers of Philadelphia Hall of Fame in 2007.

Tom Brookshier died of cancer on January 29, 2010.

IRV CROSS

T hanks to the power of television, most people know Irv Cross from his days on the *NFL Today* pregame CBS television show. Cross and his sidekicks, Brent Musburger and Phyllis George (later Jayne Kennedy) entertained fans prior and during Sunday NFC action.

Born in Hammond, Indiana, Irv was an outstanding athlete during his high school days, winning numerous athletic honors. At Northwestern University he played fullback and defensive and offensive end, and earned honorable mention All-Big Ten honors.

A seventh-round draft choice of the Philadelphia Eagles in 1961, Cross was quickly recognized as one of the hardest-hitting defensive backs in pro football.

"I didn't know much about Philadelphia," Cross said. "Oh, I knew about the Liberty Bell and Independence Hall and Betsy Ross, but other than that I had no idea at all. When you first come to town, you're just trying to make the team up in Hershey.

"I had never seen a row house before."

But Cross quickly adapted and earned his spot on the team. Of course, it was a team that had won the NFL Championship the year before.

"Not everyone has the chance to play on a championship team," he said. "But we were the defending champions. There is an air of

Photo courtesy of the Philadelphia Eagles

#27 · IRV CROSS
Northwestern • Hgt: 6-1 • Wgt: 190 • Born: July 27, 1939

Position: Defensive Back
Nine-Year NFL Career
Eagles Six Years (1961-1965, 1969)

confidence that we'd win every game. All we had to do was play our game and we'd win.

"It was a veteran, mature team. A confident, close team. We were more like a family than a team. The fans were so energized when you did well. It was also very surprising to me how 60,000 fans could boo in unison. It would like an orchestra, or a choir directed by someone who would cue the fans. Boos would resonate through the stadium."

An excellent player, Cross was rarely if ever the brunt of the adverse fan reaction. But as the team began to slip, it was harder to maintain that strong team outlook.

"At first with our team, the boos didn't bother us," Cross said. "If we played well, the fans supported us. If we didn't, we deserved to get booed. But into the mid-'60s, we had a lot of guys hurt and there was a lot of tension on the team. As long as you were playing well, it's okay. But you didn't have as much sympathy for a teammate who isn't doing well when you are losing."

During his career, Irv Cross was part of history a couple of times. He was part of the game where the nickel defense was invented. In game preparation for Mike Ditka and the Chicago Bears, defensive coach and future Eagles head coach Jerry Williams invented a scheme where the middle linebacker came out of the game, to be replaced by a fifth defensive back. The defensive coach of the Bears, George Allen, later upgraded the concept, and as head coach of the Los Angeles Rams, traded for Eagles linebacker Maxie Baughan and Cross.

"I loved playing for the Rams," Cross said. "Coach Allen was all about 100 percent a defensive coach. It was wonderful. You go into the defensive huddle and see the Fearsome Foursome on your side—Lamar Lundy, Rosey Grier, Merlin Olsen and Deacon Jones. It was like I died and went to heaven. We had an awesome defense, but my heart was still in Philadelphia."

Cross returned to the Eagles as a player/coach in 1969 under new head coach Jerry Williams. He also hosted a top-rated radio program and began a career in television that eventually landed him a job on the *NFL Today* for CBS.

Irv began his career at CBS as a game analyst and was co-host and expert commentator on the emmy award-winning *NFL Today* show for 15 years. Besides football, Irv covered a variety of sports for CBS, including track and field, gymnastics and the NBA.

"Working on the *NFL Today* was huge," he said. "We all just kind of fell into it. But the three of us had tremendous chemistry. We got along on the set and really liked each other off camera. We had great times preparing for the shows. We all had distinct responsibilities and had to focus.

"The idea was that we wanted people to have a better idea of what they were going to see in the game. Our job was to educate as well as entertain. We reported the news as opposed to becoming the news."

After a long and successful run with CBS, Cross became the director of athletics at Idaho State before moving on to director of athletics at Macalester College in St. Paul. He has also enjoyed time as a sportscaster, public speaker, community leader, and family man.

Irv Cross has fond memories of Philadelphia and hopes that fans will remember his efforts on the field, not just in the broadcasting booth.

"I really miss Philadelphia after I visit there," he said. "I have a great appreciation for the east coast and the state of Pennsylvania. Philadelphia is a city of fond memories for me. The fans are very loyal. I hope they'll think of me as a guy who did the best he could. I was always honest and fair with people and tried to treat everyone well, like I'd like to be treated.

"The sports experience is a good one because it makes you a better person."

Irv has been active in numerous community and charitable projects. Causes that are closest to his heart include youth, the homeless and abused women and children. He has served on the board of trustees of the NCAA Foundation and as chairman of the Educational Advisory Panel for Pop Warner Little Scholars; advisor to the Department of Agriculture for Team Nutrition; past advisor to the President's Council on Physical Fitness and Sports' Youth Fitness Committee; past member of the Board of Highland School, Youth for Tomorrow, and Chadwick International; and former chairman of the American Running and Fitness Association.

Cross was the recipient of the Pete Rozelle Radio-Television Award in 2009. The award, given annually by the Pro Football Hall of Fame, recognizes "long-time exceptional contributions to radio and television in professional football."

BRIAN DAWKINS

A ll you really need to know about the type of player that standout defensive star Brian Dawkins was during his brilliant 16-year NFL career is to understand his nickname. He had the moniker, "Weapon X," a code name for the Marvel character Wolverine, the comic book hero known for relentless aggression.

Drafted in the second round of the 1996 draft, Dawkins had an outstanding college career at Clemson University. In his three years as a starter at free safety, he accumulated 247 tackles and 11 interceptions. It didn't take him long to begin making a name for himself in Philadelphia.

He quickly replaced Eric Zumalt as the Eagles starting free safety, a post he maintained for his entire tenure in Philadelphia. He teamed with Troy Vincent and Bobby Taylor to form one of the most dominant secondaries in the NFL. During his thirteen years in Midnight Green, Dawkins averaged 55 tackles a season, had 21 sacks, 34 interceptions and 33 forced fumbles. Not surprising, he was a nine-time Pro Bowl selection, is a member of the Philadelphia Eagles 75th Anniversary team and is also a member of the NFL 2000s All-Decade Team. Nor is it surprising that his name is often mentioned when the subject arises regarding players who will be eligible for the Hall of Fame in Canton, Ohio for the first time in 2017.

Photo courtesy of the Philadelphia Eagles

#20 · BRIAN DAWKINS
Clemson • Hgt: 6-0 • Wgt: 210 • Born: October 13, 1973

Position: Safety
16-year NFL Career
Eagles 13 Years (1996-2008)

"He is the best safety in franchise history," said Ray Didinger. "He is probably the best defensive back in franchise history. Even when he was just a kid, you could see that he had great quickness when the ball was in the air. He was able to close in on a ball so quickly, from point A to point B.

"His ability to blitz from the safety position was something else that made him stand out. Blitzing is very much a timing thing. Some guys can just anticipate and have a sense of when to take off. Dawkins had that. Ray Rhodes (Dawkins' first Eagles coach) and Emmitt Thomas (his first NFL position coach) were a little distrustful of young players. But when Andy Reid came in and brought in Jim Johnson (the late defensive coordinator), he saw that they had a uniquely talented player."

Dawkins was not only the defensive leader of the Eagles, but he also was a tremendous fan favorite who would not only fire up his teammates, but his pre-game antics got Philadelphia's fanatical football fans in a frenzy. There were numerous game and individual highlights during his career in Philadelphia, but every game he played was a game in which his presence was always felt.

In the NFC Championship game of 2004, when the Eagles defeated the Atlanta Falcons to advance to the Super Bowl, it was Dawkins who had numerous key hits as well as an interception of a Michael Vick pass. The disappointment of the Birds' 27-24 loss in that game did nothing to take away from his defensive dominance, which continued throughout his time with the team.

His career in Philadelphia came to an end following the Eagles loss to the Arizona Cardinals in the NFC Championship game of 2008. After a pedestrian first half of the season, the Eagles caught fire and were again just one game away from the Super Bowl. In spite of his best efforts, their season ended one game short of the ultimate goal. And in spite of his incredible career as an Eagle, Dawkins signed a five-year multi-million-dollar pact with the Denver Broncos.

Denver welcomed Dawkins, and his excellent play and unquestioned leadership continued in Denver. In his first year as a Bronco, Dawkins had 95 tackles, three forced fumbles and a pair of interceptions. But he was hampered by injuries the following two seasons, playing in 25 games with 93 tackles, seven forced fumbles and one interception. Father Time and his ferocious style of play had finally caught up with No. 20.

In April of 2012, Dawkins announced that he was retiring from the game he loved. The Eagles signed him to a one-day contract so he could retire as a Bird. His number was retired by the team later that season.

"Before Brian, the safety was not a very important player in the NFL," said Ray Didinger. "But that changed with Andy Reid and Jim Johnson. They built the defense around Dawkins' skills. Other teams saw that and you started to see guys like Ed Reed and Troy Polamalu come in. These guys were football descendants of Brian Dawkins.

"Safeties have now become marquee players on the defense and he started it. He made a great impact around the league."

Brian Dawkins now serves as an analyst for ESPN.

RANDY LOGAN

L oyal Eagles fans who appreciated the efforts of strong safety Randy Logan can probably thank tight end Charles Young for getting him in Philadelphia. When the Birds brass asked Young who the best strong safety he played against in college was, the first-round pick named Randy Logan. The rest is history.

The Eagles made Logan, an All-American in 1972 at Michigan their third-round draft pick. Eleven years later, he retired as a fan favorite who intercepted 23 passes in his career and played in a Super Bowl. Not bad for a guy who thought he was going to be drafted by the Los Angeles Rams.

"I thought an arrangement had been made with the Los Angeles Rams," Logan said. "I knew nothing of Philadelphia at all. As much as I was into football, it never dawned on me that I'd go there. I was certain I'd go to a west coast team or a team in the southwest. But when I was drafted by the Eagles, I was happy and elated to be given the chance to play."

While he made an immediate impression with his aggressive play, professional football was not Randy Logan's only adjustment. He went from a program at Michigan where the team rarely lost to the 1973 Eagles, who were to go 5-8-1.

AP/WWP

#41 · RANDY LOGAN
Michigan • Hgt: 6-1 • Wgt: 192 • Born: May 1, 1951

Position: Strong Safety
11-Year NFL Career
Eagles 11 Years (1973-1983)

"During my four years at Michigan, we may have lost three or four games," he said. "The only games I remember losing were to Stanford in the Rose Bowl and a couple of games to Ohio State. It was a winning program. In Philadelphia that wasn't the case. I was always very hard on myself, and it was quite an adjustment with all the losing.

"But just being a professional football player was a great thrill. It was a great feeling. I enjoyed playing under Mike McCormick, but as a team we wanted to win. Then Dick Vermeil came in and he was persistent and determined. We turned things around, and winning was really exciting, a great feeling.

"Everybody enjoyed winning. It was like college again for me. Leonard Tose, who used to own the team, would take the team down to Bookbinder's on Monday evenings to celebrate a victory. The team really enjoyed that."

As is often the case, winning beget winning, and the Birds flew to New Orleans for an appearance in Super Bowl XV. Although they had beaten the Oakland Raiders handily during the regular season, it was all Raiders on Super Bowl Sunday.

"We built up to the Super Bowl over the course of a few years," Logan said. "We saw it coming as we jelled as a team, each year getting stronger and stronger. Coach Vermeil kept everything very positive. He was the master in building confidence in one another and the team. All the credit goes to him for bringing us trust and confidence. It was an awesome year.

"The Super Bowl was very disappointing to lose. Thinking about it now, it all happened so fast. It was there and then it was gone. A lot of people think that we were too tight. But Coach Vermeil did what he had done with us all year long. The magnitude of the practices was intensified. We got there through hard work and practice. If we had changed how we prepared and lost, it would have been worse. We just did what we always did.

"I was disappointed for losing, but it was a real pleasure having the opportunity to participate in it. A lot of colleagues I know never had the chance to play in that game. I feel like I was blessed."

Randy Logan was a popular player appreciated by the fans as well as his teammates.

"He was a quiet, low-key kind of guy," said former Eagles center Guy Morriss. "Randy was a tremendous football player who didn't say a whole lot. A good, solid player week in and week out who had a great attitude."

Those sentiments were echoed by another former offensive lineman, Jerry Sizemore.

"Randy was a real quiet individual," he said. "A very solid individual who was very firm in his religions life. On the football field, he would knock you out. He would come up and really force the play. What a fierce competitor. But all you ever got out of him was a smile."

Logan retired following the 1983 season although he nearly signed with the USFL Michigan Panthers. He went to work for Electronic Data Systems in the Detroit area for 11 years in the accounts payable department. But after a business trip to Philadelphia, Randy Logan and his wife decided that they wanted to return to the City of Brotherly Love.

He has served as the assistant dean of student affairs for St. Gabriel's Hall, a reform school in Audubon, Pennsylvania, dealing with youth between the ages of 11 and 18 who have been sent to the school rather than prison. For many, it's their last chance to walk the straight and narrow.

"It's very rewarding," he said. "We decide if they are ready to reenter society. We have some victories and some losses. We enjoy the victories, and the losses break our hearts. The most rewarding part is that a whole lot of them get their lives turned around and are very thankful. We thank God.

"I tried to always do my best in every situation, help people and be a team member. You get back what you give. My philosophy has been to give in a manner in which the good Lord has told us. You try to care and love and give back. There is great return in doing God's will and treating others as you would like to be treated."

AL NELSON

During his nine-year tenure with the Philadelphia Eagles, cornerback Al Nelson enjoyed but one winning season, when the Birds went 9-5 in 1966. Coming from a successful college program at Cincinnati, losing was a difficult adjustment for Nelson to make.

"We only had the one winning season during the time I played," he said. "We went to the Runner-Up Bowl in Miami against Baltimore. I came from a winning program in college. I was a successful individual. But football is only fun if you win. The seasons become long and laborous. It's much more difficult when you lose. I came to Philadelphia as a third-round draft choice. I was a starter and had some limited success. I really enjoyed Philadelphia. There is nothing bad to say about it. I'm just sorry we didn't win more games."

Actually, Al Nelson was a very successful college running back, finishing third in the nation in rushing. In spite of his dreams of being an NFL running back, the Eagles liked his athleticism and switched him to the defensive backfield. He started immediately and became one of the most dependable players in his era.

In his time with the Eagles, Al Nelson nabbed 13 interceptions in a defense that was not geared toward individual accomplishment. In those days, the whole concept was to control the offense.

AP Photo/Bill Ingraham

#26 · AL NELSON
Cincinnati • Hgt: 5-11 • Wgt: 190 • Born: October 27, 1943

Position: Corner Back
Nine-Year NFL Career
Eagles Nine Years (1965-1973)

"It was a team where I couldn't gamble a lot as a cornerback," he said.

"Everything defensively was geared to funneling the receiver to the middle of the field."

One of Nelson's jobs on those dismal Eagle teams was to return kickoffs, which he did exceedingly well. The team gave up plenty of points, so Nelson had lots of practice bringing back kicks. A speedy runner with excellent moves, he averaged nearly 27 yards per kick off return during his career, giving the Eagles faithful something to cheer about. As the type of player who competed on every play, Nelson was well liked by the fans and probably got as many cheers as any player on the team.

"I played hard," he said. "Losing as much as we did, it wasn't easy. At the same time, I enjoyed my time there. The fans were tough. But if you can play nine years in a town like Philadelphia on a losing team, either you were terrible or they just couldn't find anyone better. But I played hard and played with passion."

His career ended following the 1973 season and Al Nelson went to work, primarily involved in government positions. He was employed by the Delaware County Division of Parks and Recreation as special assistant in community affairs. He is retired from his post in Harrisburg as a counselor working with youth programs after more than 30 years.

Leaving professional football was difficult, but Nelson was prepared to make the change.

"After I was released by the Eagles, I went to the Bears," he said. "But that didn't work out. They wanted to pay me half of what I was making in Philadelphia. It was a tough transition from football. Real tough. But I managed because I had always worked during the off season. I had no trouble adapting to a nine-to-five job. I was a disciplined type of athlete. So I was able to make the transition."

But Al Nelson is remembered as a fine player by the fans and as a great teammate.

"Al was really fast," said Leroy Keyes, who played in the defensive backfield with Nelson. "He is a super person. I really enjoyed playing in the secondary with him. He always gave you a hand and made a point to tell you what kind of car you wanted to drive."